DATE DUE

Demco, Inc. 38-293

THE Saint Peter principle

Paul W. Powell

BROADMAN PRESS
Nashville, Tennessee

BV
4501.2
P59
S25
1982
c.4

© Copyright 1982 • Broadman Press.

All rights reserved.

4252-99

ISBN: 0-8054-5299-0

Scripture verses marked NASB are from the *New American Standard Bible.* Copyright © The Lockman Foundation, 1960, 1962, 1963, 1971, 1972, 1973, 1975. Used by permission.

Scripture verses marked RSV are from the Revised Standard Version of the Bible, copyrighted 1946, 1952, © 1971, 1973.

Scripture verses marked TEV are from the *Good News Bible,* the Bible in Today's English Version. Old Testament; copyright © American Bible Society 1976; New Testament: copyright © American Bible Society 1966, 1971, 1976. Used by permission.

Dewey Decimal Classification: 248.4

Subject heading: CHRISTIAN LIFE // PETER, APOSTLE

Library of Congress Catalog Card Number: 81-067372

Printed in the United States of America

Dedicated
to
BOB ROGERS

Partner
Friend
Brother

Foreword

When John Bunyan had written *The Pilgrim's Progress,* he showed the manuscript to several friends. Without exception they informed him that, while they were impressed by the work, he should not venture to publish it. Convinced that he had been inspired by God to write this allegory, Bunyan scorned all advice and published the piece—and how glad we are that he did!

Not only did Bunyan provide the world with one of the greatest religious classics of all times, he brought home to us in unforgettable fashion that the Christian life is a pilgrimage. Paul Powell, in his book *The Saint Peter Principle,* clearly describes the path of the pilgrimage to Christian maturity.

Any book from the pen of Dr. Powell will be treasured, but this one which deals with the foundation and the superstructure of the Christian life should be required reading for every leader. In fifteen chapters entitled: Dedication, Risks, Faith, Self-Denial, Involvement, Reconciliation, Influence, Grace, Forgiveness, Watchfulness, Humility, Determination, Repentance, Power, and Endurance, the author makes it clear that only as we realize our full life in Christ can we live in right relationship to God and to society.

With admirable skill, the author deals with the tragedy of potential unfulfilled. Realizing that many are inspired to commitment, but somehow never reach Christian maturity in their knowledge or character, Dr. Powell sets forth, by regular references to Peter, the virtues which make human life great! The Apostle Peter, as mentioned in the Gospels, is an entirely different person from the mature Peter of the Epistles, and the same grace that was available to Peter is also available to us.

JAMES LANDES
Executive Director
Baptist General Convention of Texas

Contents

Introduction 9
1. DEDICATION:
   The Key to Achievement 11
2. RISKS:
   The Waste of Underemployment 20
3. FAITH:
   Rocks Don't Have to Sink 31
4. SELF-DENIAL:
   From Spirituality to Carnality 42
5. INVOLVEMENT:
   From Inspiration to Perspiration 50
6. RECONCILIATION:
   Receiving and Giving Forgiveness 60
7. INFLUENCE:
   An Offense to None 71
8. GRACE:
   The Bottom Line of Discipleship 81
9. FORGIVENESS:
   Initial and Continual Cleansing 91
10. WATCHFULNESS:
    The Sifting of Satan 101
11. HUMILITY:
    Overcome by Overconfidence 112
12. DETERMINATION:
    Failure Doesn't Have to be Final 122
13. REPENTANCE:
    The Gospel of the Second Chance 132
14. POWER:
    A Rock-Man at Last 141
15. ENDURANCE:
    The Peter Principle and Saint Peter 149

Introduction

Do you feel that you have never reached your highest potential in either your character or your career? Does your life lack eternal significance? Do you wonder at times if you are wasting your life on things that do not really matter?

If so, there is hope and help for you. Come walk with me through the life of Simon Peter the apostle and see how God took this obscure, unstable fisherman, who was wasting his life on the Sea of Galilee, and made him the dynamic, dependable leader of the early New Testament church. Watch him as his weak and unpredictable character is radically changed by the Lord, and he becomes the solid, rock-like kind of man Jesus could build on.

Observe him as he gives up the security of the small fishing outfit he was running so he could devote his life to catching men for God. As you see Christ mold Peter into the man he had it in him to become, you will be able to see your own possibilities for change and spiritual achievement. What Jesus did in Peter's life, he can also do in yours. If you will begin to follow Jesus as Peter did, the Master can lift you to your highest potential.

This truth is so basic to life that I call it the "Saint Peter Principle." The principle, simply stated, is this: *Through commitment to Christ, a person can rise to his highest level of competency in both what he is and what he does.*

Don't confuse *The Saint Peter Principle* with *The Peter Prin-*

ciple, made popular a few years ago by Dr. Lawrence J. Peter and Raymond Hull. They taught in their book that in a corporate hierarchy every employee tends to rise to his highest level of incompetence; that is, if a man is a good salesman, he is promoted to sales manager, a position which he may not be able to handle. Employees are continaully moved up the ladder of success until they are eventually promoted beyond their ability. In short, the cream rises until it sours. They felt that every thriving organization is characterized by this accumulation of dead wood at the top.

While their book was a tongue-in-cheek presentation, there was enough truth in it to capture the imagination of the American public and make it a number-one best-seller.

This book is no tongue-in-cheek presentation. What I am talking about works. Peter is an eternal example of what God can do anywhere, anytime, with any person. I have seen it work in my own life and in the lives of countless other people. You need not stop short of your potential. You, too, can develop into everything God wants you to be in both your character and your career if you will apply the Saint Peter Principle to your life.

1
DEDICATION
The Key to Achievement

The differences among people are not so much in their abilities as in their commitments. It is the object and degree of your commitment that will ultimately determine your success or failure in life.

It is my conviction that until you commit your life to Jesus Christ you can never achieve your highest potential. Apart from Christian discipleship, you can never become what you have it in you to be. This is the heart of the Saint Peter Principle. The truth of this can be clearly seen in the life and experiences of Saint Peter, the first of the twelve apostles of Jesus Christ.

Peter was an ordinary fisherman on the Sea of Galilee until he met Christ. But once he recognized Jesus as the Messiah and began to follow him, his whole life began to change. With that commitment, he launched out on his journey of becoming what he was capable of being in both his character and his career.

Peter's spiritual development actually began with his brother, Andrew. Andrew had been a disciple of John the Baptist when Andrew first learned that Jesus was the Messiah, God's anointed king.

Andrew immediately found his brother and told him of his discovery. Then the two of them went to meet Jesus. When they arrived, Jesus looked at Simon with a deep, penetrating gaze and said, "I know you; your name is Simon. But from now your new name will be Peter" (John 1:42, author's paraphrase). The name "Peter" is an Aramaic word which means "stone" or "rock." Jesus was saying, "From now on we are going to call you Rocky. You will be a rock-like man."

This new name was a prophetic statement of what grace would make out of this weak, vacillating, impetuous man. It foretold his new character. This is where God always begins his work in our lives. Before he does a work through us, he always does a work in us, because doing results from being. Service flows from character.

Character, after all, is the real measure of achievement in life. Wealth, fame, place, and power are no measure of success whatever. The true measure of success is not what we have or what we do but what we are.

The statement of Jesus about Peter must have been a surprise to everyone who heard it and who knew Simon. He was anything but a rock-like man. He was more like shifting sand. He was unstable, unpredictable, and fickle. His moods changed as quickly as the wind on the Sea of Galilee where he fished for a living. At one moment, the sea could be dead calm. The next moment it could be whirling and turbulent, lashing in fury.

If you had asked people about Peter, they probably would have said, "Oh, yes, I know old Simon. He is a good sort, but he's no leader. You can't build on him."

But Jesus does not look at us as other people do. He sees not only what we are; he also sees what we can become. He views not only the actualities in people, but also the possibilities. Jesus looked at Peter and saw in him the possibility of his becoming a strong, predictable, steadfast man. He saw in him the capacity to develop into the solid, Gibraltar-like man on whom He could depend and build. So he gave Peter this new name which would be a constant reminder of what the Lord expected him to become. The confidence of Jesus must

DEDICATION: The Key to Achievement

have gripped Peter's soul and must also have been a mighty force in his spiritual development.

Following Jesus was the turning point in Peter's life. The day he recognized, accepted, and began to follow Jesus as God's anointed king, he started to become like a rock. He was on the road to achieving his highest spiritual potential. In the years to come he would courageously stand and proclaim the gospel on the day of Pentecost. He would resist the threats and intimidations of religious and political leaders. He would spearhead the spread of the gospel among his own people. Many biblical scholars believe that Peter dictated the notes from which Mark would write the first gospel, all under the inspiration of the Spirit. He would encourage others to be faithful in suffering and vigilant in temptation. And he would eventually give his life for the cause of Christ. What a record of service! But it all had its beginning when he committed himself to Jesus as the Messiah.

From that day forward, his life took on a new direction, a new destiny, and a new dimension. Under this new loyalty to Jesus, all things were made new.

Today Jesus challenges us as he did Peter, "Give your life to me, and I will make you what you have it in you to be." You do not have to stay the way you are. You can move on to greater spiritual heights if you will allow Jesus to take you from where you are to where your full potential is.

How Jesus Sees Us

How can commitment to Christ bring us to our highest level of achievement? It is because of his omniscience. His first words to Peter showed that he already knew everything about the future apostle.

The word *beheld* which John uses to describe the way Jesus looked on Peter suggests an intense and concentrated gaze. It is the kind of look that sees beyond the surface of life and reads a person's heart. When Jesus first looked at Simon he saw his innermost being and perceived not only what he was but what he could become. Jesus alone has the perception to see our possibilities. That is why Christ can propel us to our highest potential. He sees the hidden potential within us. He sees what others overlook and what even we cannot see in ourselves.

George Washington Carver was one of America's greatest scientists. Among his many other achievements, he discovered over three hundred different uses for the peanut. Born in slavery, he was weak and sickly. Slave thieves, seeing little value in him, traded him back to his master for a race horse.

Jerome Hines, the great opera singer, was kicked out of junior high school glee club because the instructor said he could not carry a tune.

Thomas Edison was a giant among us. He patented over 1,093 inventions, including the phonograph, the microphone, the incandescent light bulb, the mimeograph machine, the medical fluoroscope, the nickel alkali battery, and moving pictures. Yet when he was seven years old, his school teacher gave him up as a hopeless case. He heard her tell the inspector that he was "addled" and that it was useless for him to attend school any longer.

Winston Churchill was often called "the man of the century." No one holds a greater claim to that title. His talents as a soldier, statesman, orator, and world leader almost defy belief. No other man was more instrumental in preserving our democratic way of life than he because of his leadership through the bleak, crucial days of World War II.

However, as Churchill was growing up, people called him a troublesome boy. He was redheaded, freckle-faced, and had a snub nose. He had an impediment of speech, a combination of stammer and lisp. Yet, he was uncommonly self-assured, obstinate, and arrogant.

DEDICATION: The Key to Achievement

He hated school and was constantly in trouble with his teachers. At the age of twelve, he was sent to Harrow. There he was far and away the worst pupil. In four-and-a-half years he never rose above the bottom of his class. "That lad couldn't have gone through Harrow," a contemporary remarked. "He must have gone under it." No one, not even his own parents, knew what was inside that boy. All they could see was an obviously untalented lad who had no prospect of going to Oxford and ever being good enough to become a lawyer.

Albert Einstein was the most eminent scientist of our age. He was a genius whose ideas reshaped modern scientific thinking. He described relativity and heralded the atomic age. It was largely through his involvement in the "Manhattan Project" that the atomic bomb was developed. More than anyone else, he made space exploration possible—and also gave impetus to a host of today's electronic gadgetry such as the electric eye and television.

Yet in his earlier years, Einstein showed no obvious signs of genius. He did not begin talking until the age of three! In high school he bristled at the inflexible system of rote learning and the drill-sergeant manner of his teachers. He often annoyed them with his rebellious attitude. Said one, "He will never amount to anything." At the age of sixteen, he dropped out of high school. In time, his family moved to Switzerland, and he decided to enroll in the famed Swiss Federal Institute of Technology in Zurich. But he failed the entrance exam. He went back to high school for an additional year of study and was then admitted to the institute.

Still, Einstein's rebellion continued. He cut lectures, read what he pleased, tinkered in school labs, and incurred the wrath of his teachers. One of them, mathematician Hermann Minkowski, even called him a "lazy dog." Another unnamed professor called him *Dumbkopf*—"dumb head."

Having antagonized his professors, Einstein failed to obtain a university teaching post. He eked out a living by doing calculations for an astronomer, tutoring, and substituting as a teacher.

Leonard Bernstein, the great composer, says that when he was young his father strenuously opposed his going into music. And he says, "If you were to ask my father today if he opposed this he would not deny it, but he would rationalize by saying, 'How was I to know that he was a Leonard Bernstein?' "

The truth of the matter is that we cannot know what possibilities are in a person. But the Lord does know. And it is because of his omniscience and perception that he is able to spur us on to our maximum potential.

How Jesus Handles Us

Because Jesus senses what we can become, he shows an amazing patience in helping us to grow into it. Peter did not become a rock overnight. No one does. We must beware of shortcuts to character. Thank God for instantaneous salvation, but be wary of instantaneous holiness. I believe that it does not ordinarily come that way. It is most often the result of a long and painful process.

We need emphasis on that grueling process today. We have too many "celebrities" and not enough servants. We have "ninety-day wonders" that flash across the scene of time and then disappear. Before God works through a person, he works in a man, because the work we do is an outgrowth of the lives we live. Service flows from character, and that takes time. Jesus spent thirty years preparing for three years of ministry. God prepares us for what he is preparing for us.

The Lord had to knock a lot of nonsense out of Peter. Following him through the next years, you will discover him in one instance declaring that Jesus is the Christ, the Son of the living God, and in the next breath trying to turn Jesus away

DEDICATION: The Key to Achievement

from His God-appointed mission of dying for the sins of the world. In one moment, he has enough faith to walk on water. In the next moment, he has so many fears and doubts that he sinks. At the Last Supper he boasts of his loyalty to Christ, and before the night is over denies his Master three times. Throughout the slow, painful process, Jesus never loses faith in or patience with Peter. Even though Jesus knows all along that Peter will eventually fail Him, He also knows that Peter will recover and become the useful servant.

Once someone came to Michelangelo while he was chipping away with his chisel at a huge, shapeless piece of rock. The man asked the sculptor what he was doing. "I am releasing the angel that is imprisoned in this marble," he answered. Jesus is the Master Sculptor who sees the hidden potential within us and patiently chips away at those flaws that hinder us from achieving our highest and best. And if we will keep following Jesus, he will gradually change us into what we ought to be.

How Jesus Changes Us

"But," some people say, "you can't change human nature." That's right! We can't, but Christ can. No person's character is so obstinately rooted in evil or enslaved by habit that Christ can't change it.

John declares of Jesus, "He came unto his own, and his own received him not. But as many as received him, to them gave he power to become the sons of God" (John 1:11-12).

Power to become—that's what we need. And Jesus alone can supply it. Without his life-changing power, our character would be hopelessly set.

A few years ago, we had a terrible ice storm in our city. Transformers were out, and power lines were down everywhere. Without electricity, many of our people had to heat their homes with their fireplaces and light them with kerosene lamps.

It's a strange feeling to live in a house that has every piece of electrical equipment one could want—lights, heater, stove, refrigerator, washer, dryer, vacuum cleaner—everything except power.

That's the way our lives are without Christ. We may have everything—charm, looks, personality, education, ambition, and opportunity—everything except the power to become. And ultimately the power to become is the power to change. Jesus not only sees our potential and works patiently with us, but he also gives us the power to become all that God wants us to be.

The apostle Paul, who himself was an example of this life-transforming power, said, "I can do all things through Christ which strengtheneth me" (Phil. 4:13).

Recently a friend confessed that he had never been very good in English. He had always encountered problems with punctuation. Lately, he said, he had discovered that he also had punctuation problems in his spiritual life. "For example," he said, "all of my life I have read Philippians 4:13, 'I can do all things'—period! As a result," he said, "I almost destroyed myself physically, emotionally, and spiritually. Now I have determined to stop putting punctuation marks in Scripture where they do not belong. I am learning the verse correctly, 'I can do all things *through Christ* which strengtheneth me!' "

We need to learn the same lesson. Poor spiritual punctuation can rob us of his power and cause us to trust in our own resources alone.

You may have tried a thousand times to change on your own, only to fail dismally in every instance. And you will keep on failing until you have the strength of Christ in you. You cannot change your character on your own, but through Christ all things are possible.

DEDICATION: The Key to Achievement

When he comes into your life, he enables you to become all that he wants you to be and all you are capable of being. Your character can reach its highest potential when Christ is pouring his power into you. Just as surely as Christ changed Simon into a rock, so he can change you and me. That's the heart of the "Saint Peter Principle."

The key is commitment! Begin to follow Christ with all of your heart now, and it will be the beginning of a new life for you.

2
RISKS
The Waste of Underemployment

Recently, I talked with a young man that I had not seen in several years. The last time I saw him he was in college preparing to be a minister of music. He had one of the most beautiful bass voices I have ever heard and also an unusual ability to communicate with people as he sang. So I asked him, "What are you doing now?" He ducked his head and said almost apologetically, "Oh, I'm just raising dogs." As I walked away I shook my head and thought, "What a waste! A voice like that, and all he is doing is raising dogs."

There is, of course, nothing wrong with raising dogs—unless you can sing like he can. Then it is clearly a waste—the waste of underemployment. It occurs to me that there is more than one way to waste a life. We can waste our lives through riotous living, like the Prodigal Son, or we can waste them at a task which is beneath our ability. The world is full of people who are underemployed. They are capable of much more than they are doing—and much more than they are being.

Through commitment to Jesus Christ we can all reach our highest potential, not only in our character, but also in our career. This is the second dimension of the "Saint Peter Principle." Jesus' first concern is our character—what we are. But he is also concerned about our career—what we do. If we will follow him, he will help us achieve our highest level of competence in both areas.

This truth, like that of Chapter 1, can also be seen in the life

RISKS: The Waste of Underemployment

of the apostle Peter. One day, as Jesus walked by the Sea of Galilee and saw Peter and his brother Andrew fishing, he called them, "Follow me, and I will make you fishers of men" (Matt. 4:18-19). And immediately they left their nets and began to follow him. In this encounter, Jesus was calling Peter to new employment—to a new career that would give eternal significance to his life.

This is not the first time Jesus and Peter had met. Their first encounter had been several months, perhaps even a year, earlier. At that first meeting, Jesus gave Simon his new name, Peter. From that day forward, Peter was committed to Jesus. He had become Jesus' disciple.

After that first meeting, Peter and Andrew returned to the Sea of Galilee and their fishing trade. Now, several months later, Jesus issued this call to them. It was a call to abandon everything, their occupation (a lucrative business), their relatives, their home, and friends—and to devote themselves to preaching the gospel. It was a call to fellowship and to service.

Peter was a fisherman by trade. There is nothing wrong with that. Thank God for fishermen. They help to feed the world. However, Simon was capable of more than being a fisherman. He had the potential of becoming a great preacher and leader. He would one day be at the forefront of the cause of Christ. He would preach on the day of Pentecost, and three thousand people would be saved. He would serve as an oral source for his nephew Mark's Gospel, and he would eventually write the two epistles in the New Testament that bear his name. He would become one of the most influential men in all of history.

If Simon had stayed on the Sea of Galilee, none of the above would have happened. What a terrible waste it would have been for Simon to spend his life dragging the Sea of Galilee when he could be discipling the world!

Jesus, seeing his possibilities, issued Peter this call, "Follow me, and I will *make* you to become a fisher of men" (see Matt. 4:19). Jesus used the figure of his old occupation to illustrate the new work he had for Peter to do. He would spend his days catching men out of the troubled sea of sin. He would catch them for God.

The word *make* is a construction term that is oftentimes used to describe the creative act of God. It is the same word Jesus used when he said, "In the beginning God *made* them male and female" (Matt. 19:4). It is the same word the apostle Paul used when he said, "and God *made* of one blood all men who dwell in the face of the earth" (Acts 17:26). Jesus was teaching here that just as God "made" Adam and Eve in the beginning and just as he "made" of one blood all men, so he could *make* Peter to be a fisher of men.

The fact is that the creative work of God did not end in the beginning. Nor does it end at conception. It continues throughout our lives as Christians. It is still going on at this moment. So no matter what you may have made of yourself or how proud you may be of the achievements you have made, until you commit your life to Jesus and let his creative power continue to work in your life, you will never reach your greatest potential. God is still in the process of making his disciples into what he wants them to be.

With that call from Jesus, Simon's life took on an eternal dimension. He would no longer be merely existing; he would now be living a life with purpose and meaning. Life would be exciting, challenging, demanding from this day forward.

So, he immediately left his nets and began to follow Jesus. This was not blind impulse, but the deliberate surrender of a man who knew what he was doing. He made a studied decision when he decided to follow Jesus.

What Jesus did for Peter he can also do for you. He is in the business of calling people from wasted lives and second-rate commitments and giving their lives the stamp of eternity.

To find God's will and work for your life is to make life's

RISKS: The Waste of Underemployment

greatest discovery. To do God's will and work is life's greatest achievement. I know this not only from Scripture but from my own experience. If I had planned my own life, I would have cheated myself. Years ago, my ambition was nothing more than to be a worker in an oil refinery. I would have been content to work forty hours a week, to put in my thirty years of service, and then retire with a good pension. But Jesus had other plans for me. He called me into his service, and with that call he gave my life a new significance. Through his leadership, I have been able to go places and do things that I would never have dreamed possible. I would have missed the best in life if I had never heard and answered God's call.

Could it be that you are also underemployed? Are you wasting your life on some insignificant little Sea of Galilee when God has something greater for you to do? Does your life lack eternal significance? Is life stale and boring for you? If so, it may well be that you are underemployed. But it doesn't have to be that way. Through commitment to Jesus Christ, your life can take on new meaning, purpose, and direction. You can lay aside your old nets and assume a work that has eternal meaning.

But, like Peter, you must have the faith to believe, the courage to forsake your old life-style, and the determination to follow Jesus—no matter what. Through faith, forsaking, and following, you can find God's purpose for your life. Commit your life to him and let him make you into what you are capable of being.

How does Jesus make us into what he wants us to become? There are three ways: by his confidence in us, by his call to us, and by his companionship with us.

A Challenging Confidence

In his first encounter with Peter, Jesus had prophesied that Simon would become rock-like in his character. Now he promised to make him into a missionary in his career. That confidence must have gripped Peter's soul. It had to be a mighty force in his spiritual development.

Jonathan Swift wrote, "Although men are accused of not knowing their own weakness, yet perhaps few know their own strength. It is in men as in soils, where sometimes there is a vein of gold which the owner knows not of."

A part of the omniscience of Jesus is that he could spot that vein of gold in people and make them believe they were of value to God. His confidence in us helps us take the step of faith necessary to finding life at its best.

Fred Craddock tells a story that illustrates this. His family roots were in Tennessee, and one summer he and his wife went back to Gatlinburg for a vacation. One night they went to a restaurant that looks out over the Smoky Mountains, and as they were dining a distinguished-looking, older man who seemed to be the proprietor moved from table to table speaking to guests. Craddock acknowledged that he himself was a rather private person and particularly on vacation did not like to be interfered with. Thus he was somewhat resentful as the old man finally made his way to their table and began to converse.

"Where are you all from?" the old man asked.

Craddock answered, "Oklahoma."

"What do you do?"

"I teach homiletics in the graduate seminary of Phillips University."

"Oh, so you are a preacher," he said. "I have got a preacher story I need to tell you."

With that he pulled up a chair, and Craddock winced at what was to come. The old man said, "I was born just a few miles from here, across the mountain. My mother was not married at the time, and the reproach that fell on her fell on me as well. They had a name for me when I started to school,

RISKS: The Waste of Underemployment

and it was not nice. I can remember going off by myself at recess and at lunchtime because the taunts of my peers cut so deep. What was even worse was to go to town with my mother on Saturday and feel all those eyes literally piercing through me, and realize they were asking, 'Whose child is he? I wonder who his father is.'

"When I was about twelve, a new preacher came to the little church in our community, and people began to talk about his power and his eloquence. I began to go myself and was intrigued by him, although I always slipped in late and tried to get out early because I was afraid that people would say, 'What is a boy like you doing in a place like this?' But one Sunday the benediction got said quicker than I realized, and I found myself caught with lots of people crowding around the door and unable to get out. As I was waiting there, scared to death, I felt a hand on my shoulder and turned around. There stood the preacher, looking at me with those burning eyes. He said, 'Who are you, Son? Whose boy are you?' And I thought to myself, *Oh, no, here we go again.*

"But then," he said, "a smile of recognition broke across his face, and he said, 'Wait a minute. I know who you are. I see the family resemblance. You are a son of God!' And with that he patted me across the rump and said, 'Boy, you got quite an inheritance. Go and claim it!' 'That one statement,' said the old man, 'literally changed my life.' "

By this time, Craddock was utterly enthralled and asked, "Who are you?"

The old man replied, "Ben Hooper."

Then Craddock said to himself, *Ben Hooper! Oh, yes. I remember how my grandfather used to tell that on two occasions the people from Tennessee elected an illegitimate man to be their governor, and his name was Ben Hooper!*

This is the work of Jesus. He has two things to say to every one of us. First, "I know who you are. I see the family resemblance. You are a child of God." And then, like that blessed old mountain preacher, "You have a great inheritance. Go and claim it."

It is this confidence of Jesus that starts us on the road to being what we ought to be.

How to Know God's Will

God's confidence in us then issues forth into a call to us. As surely as he called Peter to be a fisher of men, so he calls all people to their best. That call represents the will of God for our lives. We understand how Jesus could walk by the Sea of Galilee and call Peter. But how does God call us today? How can we know the will of God for our lives?

First, God reveals his will to us by *impressions*. Peter Marshall spoke of a "tap on the shoulder." Others call it "an inner light." Call it what you will. God comes to us at times with impressions and convictions so strong that we just know that they are from him. If you have never experienced God speaking to you in this way, it could be that you simply did not recognize his voice when it came to you.

Second, God makes his will known to us through our *intelligence*. There are times when we pray and no clear impression comes. What are we to do then? We are to use the intelligence God gave us. If God did not expect us to use our minds, why did he give them to us? He could just as well have given us computer printouts each day. Then we wouldn't need to think at all. But he didn't. He gave us the mental machinery for making decisions, and he expects us to use it.

A. W. Tozer said,

> Some Christians walk under a cloud of uncertainty worrying about which profession they should enter, which car they should drive, which school they should attend, where they should live, and other such matters when

RISKS: The Waste of Underemployment

> their Lord has set them free to follow their own personal bent, guided only by their love for him and their fellowmen. On the surface it appears more spiritual to seek God's leading than just to go ahead and do the obvious thing. But it is not. If God gave you a watch, would you honor him by asking him for the time of day or by consulting the watch? If God gave a sailor a compass, would the sailor please God more by kneeling in a frenzy of prayer to persuade God to show him which way to go or by steering according to the compass? Except for those things that are specifically commanded or forbidden, it is God's will that we be free to exercise our own intelligent choice. The shepherd will lead the sheep, but he does not wish to decide which turf of grass the sheep will nibble. God's choice for us may not be one but any one of a score of possible choices.[1]

Apparently, he allowed the apostle Paul to plan his own missionary itinerary and interrupted it only when Paul needed to change directions. On his Second Missionary Journey, the apostle Paul planned to enter Asia when God gave him a vision in the night of a man from Macedonia. So he changed directions and went to Europe instead. Had God been leading Paul to Bithynia and then changed his mind? Or had God allowed Paul to map out his own missionary itinerary and, when he was getting off course, intervened, sending him where he was needed the most? I think God allows us to make a lot of decisions on our own, and if we are sincere and praying people, he will stop us before we can veer far off the right path.

Third, God shows us his will through *opportunities*. He opens doors of opportunity to show us what we are to do. Paul once expressed his intentions to stay in Ephesus, "For a great door and effectual is opened unto me" (1 Cor. 16:9). In spite of the obstacles, he saw the opportunities as a reason to stay. They were an indication of what he was to do.

We must always be sensitive to the leading of God and to open doors. Opportunities from God often come unannounced. The Greeks had a saying, "The gods' feet are shod in wool." God more often speaks in a whisper than a shout. If we aren't careful, we will be so busy dragging around in our little Sea of Galilee that we miss Jesus when he walks by and calls, "Come follow me."

However, a word of caution is in order. Not all opportunities are from God. Not all doors are opened by him. David's life illustrates this. God had already rejected Saul as king of Israel and had anointed David to take his place. Saul, in pursuit of David, had gone into a cave and fallen asleep. Unknown to him, David was hiding in that very cave. This provided David with a fitting opportunity to kill Saul and become the king as God had ordained. But opportunity for David did not spell permission. The advantage was not to be taken in that seemingly propitious moment. Knowing the kingdom would be his, he could wait for the right moment.

Many great people have been tempted by opportunities that did not come from God. These three things must line up—impression, intelligence, and opportunity. When they do, then we can move forward with confidence.

T. B. Maston, who was for many years professor of ethics at Southwestern Seminary, said, "The seeking mind and the willing heart and the obedient spirit cannot help but discern the will of God."

Walking with Jesus

The invitation of Jesus is always the same. It is, "Come follow me." It is a call to both forsake and to fellowship. Then day by day, experience by experience, he makes us into what we ought to be as we walk with him.

The most important thing we can do to achieve our highest

RISKS: The Waste of Underemployment

spiritual potential is to walk in constant companionship with him. This is the secret of a God-directed life. We read in Proverbs 3:5-6, "Trust in the Lord with all thine heart; and lean not unto thine own understanding. In all thy ways acknowledge him, and he shall direct thy paths." It is our responsibility to seek God. It is God's responsibility to direct us. If we will do our part, we can count on God to do his.

Paul drives this point home when he tells us to present ourselves to God that we may prove in our own experience that his will is good and acceptable and perfect (Rom. 12:1-2). There are many of us who would like to know what the will of God is before really presenting ourselves to God. We want to play it safe. We don't want to get into a situation where we can really be embarrassed. So we want to find out what we are supposed to do and where we are supposed to go in advance. But the scriptural plan is that we must present ourselves to God before we can prove through our own experience that his will is fully satisfying and that it lacks nothing necessary for completeness.

Maybe this is the crux of the whole matter. It is only when we are in fellowship with him that he comes to direct about what we ought to do. Most often God says to us, "Now that I have your will, you can have my will."

When Jesus called Peter and Andrew, "Immediately they left their nets and followed him" (Matt. 4:20, RSV). That day their lives took on a whole new meaning. The Saint Peter Principle emphasizes that by a similar surrender you can find a similar significance to your life.

In his autobiography, H. G. Wells told of a crucial moment in his life. He was apprenticed to a draper, and there seemed to be little or no future in life. There came to him one day what he called "an inward and prophetic voice: 'Get out of this trade before it is too late; at any cost, get out of it.' " He did not wait. He got out, and that is why he became H. G. Wells, the British novelist and historian. There comes a moment to decide.

May God give us the strength of decision which will save us from the tragedy of the unseized moment. May he help us to hear his voice and be willing to leave the security of our little sea. May he save us from the waste of underemployment. Do not waste your life investing it in your own ambitions. Instead, open yourself up to God. Become vulnerable to his leading, and then you will be able to ascertain his will and find an eternal significance for your life.

Note

1. A. W. Tozer, *The Tozer Pulpit,* ed. Gerald B. Smith (Harrisburg, Pennsylvania: Christian Publications, 1967).

3

FAITH
Rocks Don't Have to Sink

I recently introduced an African college student to our congregation. As I presented her, I said, "Though she is small in stature, she is a giant spiritually." I was not prepared for her first sentence.

She said, "I am not a giant. Jesus is the giant, and I hide behind him."

Elizabeth was echoing the words of the great faith-missionary Hudson Taylor, who wrote in an editorial, "All of God's giants have been weak men who did great things for God because they reckoned on his being with them."

This kind of dependence is the secret of spiritual achievement in any age and in any life. It is not self-confidence, self-effort, and self-sufficiency that lead us to our highest spiritual potential. It is faith in and dependence on Jesus Christ. Success is found in drawing from his strength, not our own.

This is basic to the Saint Peter Principle. It was a lesson Peter had to learn in order to achieve his highest potential in both character and career. And we must learn this lesson, too. Trust did not come easy to Peter. It was contrary to his nature. He considered himself a self-made and self-sufficient man. Because of his self-confidence, he often acted impulsively without thinking about what he was doing. He often committed himself beyond what he was able to achieve. He quickly jumped into a situation before he was ready for it. He had to learn his own weakness so he could draw on the strength of Jesus.

Somebody has said, "Good judgment comes from experience. Experience comes from bad judgment." That was the case with Peter. He had to make a multitude of mistakes before he learned from his own experience how much he needed to depend on the Master.

Matthew records one of these bad-judgment experiences. Jesus had moments before fed the multitudes with a few loaves of bread and a few small fish. The frenzied crowd was so excited that it wanted to seize Jesus and make him their king. This was what many first-century Jews were looking for in the Messiah; they believed that he would overthrow Rome, set up an earthly kingdom, and usher in a period of peace and prosperity where all their needs would be met. As Jesus fed them that day, they saw this potential in him.

This was not the kind of Messiah that Jesus was going to be. At this stage of their development, the disciples were more in sympathy with the crowd than their Master. Jesus saw it was dangerous to let them remain in the company of the multitudes. So he told them to get into a ship and sail for the other side of the Sea of Galilee. Then he dispersed the multitudes and went into the mountains to pray. One reason was because he was facing again the same temptation he encountered in the wilderness—to use his miraculous power to gain followers. Jesus was never free from temptation as long as he lived. So he went to be alone with God and to settle again the issue in his own heart.

Meanwhile, the disciples were having difficulty crossing the Sea of Galilee. The Sea of Galilee is thirteen miles long and seven miles wide and is usually a lovely little sheet of water. However, there are two mountain ranges to the north of it, and they form a tunnel that sometimes catches the wind and hurls it with great velocity across that once-peaceful sea. In a matter of minutes, the tranquil waters of Galilee can become turbulent and stormy. That's what had happened that night,

FAITH: Rocks Don't Have to Sink

and the disciples were caught in the middle of it.

Jesus, realizing their distress, walked on the water to help them. As they saw his image approaching, they were frightened. They believed it to be a ghost.

Jesus, sensing their fear, said, "Be of good cheer; it is I; be not afraid" (see Matt. 14:27 ff.).

Peter responded, "Lord, if it is you, then allow me to come on the water to you." That was a strange request. For the life of me, I cannot understand why Peter would ask that. I myself would have much preferred the safety of the boat. But this was typical of the impetuous Peter, who often leaped before he looked. It may well be that he thought, *If Jesus can walk on water, I can, too.*

The time had come to teach Peter, the rock man, a lesson. He had to learn that rocks can't float by themselves. So, Jesus invited Peter to come to him. Peter stepped over the side of the ship and began walking to Jesus. Everything went well until he looked down at the waves dashing against his legs and felt the spray of the sea in his face, and then he began to doubt. In that moment of doubt, he became frightened, lost faith, and started to sink. Instantly, he cried out, saying, "Lord, save me!"

Jesus stretched forth his hand, caught him, and lifted him up. Then Jesus said to him, "Oh, man of little faith, why did you doubt?" He then took Simon into the ship, and the wind ceased. And all the disciples worshiped him saying, "Truly you are the Son of God" (Matt. 14:22-33, RSV).

What Sinks Us?

The lesson of this experience is simple. Walking on water is a supernatural act. It is humanly impossible; it cannot be done apart from divine power. In the same way, walking after Christ is a supernatural act. It is not just difficult. On your own, it is impossible. In fact, it is as easy to walk on water by yourself as it is to live the Christian life by yourself.

When Jesus reproved Peter for his doubt and his little faith, he was trying to teach him the secret of spiritual achievement. Peter had to learn to trust Jesus and not himself if he were ever going to reach his highest potential in his character and his career. The Lord allowed this miracle to show that complete faith in Christ is vital to the completing of our appointed task. It was to teach him the necessity of faith in his life. If he was to become and to do, he first had to believe.

The secret of the Christian life is never a matter of self-confidence, self-effort, or self-determination. It is not believing in Jesus, receiving a do-it-yourself kit complete with instructions, and then going out and *trying as hard as you can* to live on your own. The secret is in looking to Jesus and drawing strength from him. Apart from that, we're sunk! If we focus on our own selves, our own abilities, our own talents, our own gifts, or our circumstances, we will be overcome.

The apostle Paul expressed this truth when he said, "Faithful is he that calleth you, who also will do it" (1 Thess. 5:24). The One who calls you is the One who does that to which he calls you. "For it is God which worketh in you both to will and to do of his good pleasure" (Phil. 2:13). He gives us both the will and the ability to accomplish his glorious purposes in our lives. Jesus himself is the very dynamo of all that he demands of us. If he calls us to be a rock, he is the one who will be our solidity. If he calls us to be a worldwide preacher, he is the one who with our permission will preach to men through us. He calls us, he continues to work in us, and he completes us.

This is the divine genius that saves us from the futility of self-effort. It relieves us of the burden of trying to pick ourselves up by our own bootstraps. Were it not for this divine provision, the Christian life would be a source of utter frustration and defeat. The good news would be very bad news indeed. We

FAITH: Rocks Don't Have to Sink

would be doomed to first one failure after another.

So, if we are going to reach our highest potential in character and career, we must learn to live in dependence on God. What we can become and what we can do will be limited only by our availability to him. Our faith releases God's power in our lives, and we are able to become and to do what otherwise would be impossible.

Many people have not learned that yet. That is precisely why many of them have been overcome by their circumstances and have been overwhelmed in their Christian lives. Their lives are engulfed by fear, doubts, worries, bad habits, sins, and temptations. They have tried walking after Jesus, but they have tried to do it on their own, and they have gone under.

In Peter's experience, there were three contributing factors to his defeat. Out of this defeat, he realized his helplessness and cried out to the Lord. This realization was the secret to victory for him and for us.

Distracted by Circumstances

Distractions were the first factor in Peter's defeat. His problem started when he removed his eyes from Jesus and put them on his surroundings. The Scriptures say, "When he saw the wind boisterous, he was afraid" (Matt. 14:30).

The frightful circumstances of life can cause us to take our eyes off Jesus and to put them on ourselves. Life's experiences, like the waves of the Sea of Galilee, can lash around us until we either begin to doubt the Lord or to doubt ourselves.

Satan uses many tricks to distract us from Christ. Sometimes he uses trials. The psalmist wrote that when he saw the suffering of the righteous and the prosperity of the wicked, he almost lost his footing in life (Ps. 73:1-5). The seeming inequities in life trip a lot of people. Trial and tribulation, suffering and sorrow, death and disaster often cause us to doubt our Lord and to take our eyes off him.

Material things can distract us from the Lord. I have a Korean pastor friend who was in North Korea when the Communists took over. It was only by a miracle that he escaped with his life. He came to the United States and to Texas, where he continued his education. Eventually, a little East Texas church wanted him to become their pastor. When he went for an interview with the leadership of the church, they told him that they were small and had limited resources. They had only two thousand dollars in the bank, and they had no place for a pastor to live. They suggested that an apartment could be rented for him. He told them that he liked to entertain church members and prospects in his home with a Korean meal and much preferred a house to an apartment.

So he suggested that the money be spent as a down payment on a home. They disagreed. They said to him, "You don't seem to understand. That's all the money we have. When it's gone, there is no more. We can't spend the two thousand dollars."

He replied, "If you won't spend the money, then I won't be your pastor." So he then went back to Fort Worth.

A few days later, they called again and asked him if he would reconsider being their pastor. He said, "I will if you will spend the two thousand dollars." They asked, "Why are you so intent on spending that money?" He replied, "It's because your faith is in the two thousand dollars rather than in God. If you spend the two thousand dollars, you will no longer have it to trust in, and you will have to trust in the Lord." They did as he suggested; he became their pastor and built a thriving church. There are many people like that congregation. Their spiritual vision is blurred by material things.

Disappointments can also distract us from Jesus. While awaiting execution in a Roman prison, the apostle Paul suffered many disappointments from people. Demas defected from the faith, and Alexander did him much harm. When Paul stood before Nero at the preliminary trial, all other Christians deserted him. That would be enough to discourage almost anyone. But Paul did not focus on the failures of others. He assured Timothy, "The Lord stood with me and strengthened me" (2 Tim. 4:10-18, NASB). If we focus too much on others, we will be disappointed and distracted from Christ himself. In him, there are no disappointments (Rom. 10:11).

Satan will use these and any other impediment possible to distract us from the Lord. If he succeeds in getting us to take our eyes off Christ, we're sunk.

Paralyzed by Fear

Focusing on the storms instead of the Savior caused Peter to be afraid. When his faith diminished, he lost his courage. "When he saw the wind . . . he was *afraid*" (author's italics). Fear can be disastrous. Enough of it can sink anybody, and everyone fears something.

All too many people attempt to face the storms of life with inadequate spiritual resources. Their faith is too small, and their fear is too great. We must maintain our faith if we're to keep afloat. Fear will sink us.

Faith gives us the inner resources to withstand the storms of life. Let this affirmation be our ringing cry. When our days become dreary with low-hovering clouds and our nights become darker than a thousand midnights, when the waves are dashing at our feet, let us remember that God is able to make a way out of no way, and transform dark todays into bright tomorrows. The situation may remain turbulent, but God can give us an inner calm for the storms of life.

We are not sufficient for the storms of life. We need the holy hand of Jesus to keep us up. We must cry, "Lord, save me." For when we do, he does.

How to Develop Faith

Distractions, fears, and doubts—that's the downward journey of any disciple. Jesus asked Peter, in essence, "Wherefore did you doubt, O ye of little faith?" He failed from lack of faith. Doubt sank him.

If faith is the key to Christian life, then the crucial question is, "How can I make my faith strong? How can I develop faith?"

There are several things you can do.

First, commit your life completely to Jesus Christ. Faith is not a commodity like bricks or cement. It is more like a plant. It grows. Faith is both a gift of the Spirit and a fruit of the Spirit. As we yield our lives to Jesus Christ, the Holy Spirit produces greater faith in us.

Faith is given to some people in unusual proportions. But it is also given to all of us in seed form, and like any fruit it can be cultivated and developed.

Second, read the Bible. D. L. Moody the evangelist said there was a time when he prayed for a greater faith, and he expected that it would come to him like a bolt of lightning. But it never came. Then one day he read, "Faith cometh by hearing, and hearing by the word of God" (Rom. 10:17). He said, "Up until that time my Bible had been a closed book, and I just prayed. After that I opened my Bible and began to read it, and my faith has been growing ever since."

Third, pray. Ask God to give you more faith. Remember the anguished father? He said to Jesus, "Lord, I believe, help thou mine unbelief" (Mark 9:24). Believe God as much as you can and then ask him to help you to believe him more. Ask him to stretch your faith so you can believe him completely

FAITH: Rocks Don't Have to Sink

and fully. Once your faith is stretched, it never goes back to its original size.

Fourth, use the faith you have. Many people are wanting more faith when they are not using the faith they already have. They do not realize that they already have within them the capacity to believe and to trust.

Rabbi Louis Binstock tells of a man who came into his office one day with a big problem. The rabbi said to him, "You need to put your faith in God."

"Faith, faith, faith—that's all anyone ever says to me! Have faith in God and you're going to have happiness in life and pie in the sky by-and-by. I can't believe it! Faith, faith, faith."

This businessman jumped up and was about to leave the room. Rabbi Binstock, a large man, grabbed the man by the arm and set him down in the chair. "I want you to listen to me," he said. "You are right here in the house of God. Give yourself to his grace. The storehouse of God's power is all around you. All you have to do is to use it."

And then Rabbi Binstock said to the man, "Let me tell you a story, a Chinese tale. There was once a little fish in a small river. He was swimming around underneath a boat where two Chinese men were fishing.

"One Chinese said to the other, 'Have you ever thought what we'd do without water? We couldn't live without water. We couldn't inhabit this planet without water. The crops would all dry up and die, and we'd starve to death. Without water, we couldn't exist. Water is essential to life.'

"That little fish became very excited. He had never heard that before. He began to swim around and ask some of his friends, 'Where can I get water? It's essential to life.'

"They said, 'We don't know.'

"Then the little fish went down to the big river and asked, 'Where can I get water? It's essential to life.'

"The fish there said, 'We don't know.'

"Finally the little fish swam all the way out to the ocean. In the depths of the ocean he found a very large, old fish and asked him, 'Where can I get water? It's essential to life!'

"The old fish said to the little fish, 'What do you mean—get water? You're right in the middle of water! You've been in it all the time. When you were up there in the little river, that was water. And then in the high river, that was water. And the ocean is water. It's all around you. You're right in the middle of water.'

"The little fish started swimming on his way home and thinking about what had happened. He mused, 'Water all around me all the time, and I never realized I was in the middle of it.'"

The rabbi said to the businessman, "That's the way it is with faith. You don't get faith—you use it."

When a child is born, he doesn't get arms and legs—he uses them. When you're teaching a student, he doesn't get intelligence—he uses the intelligence he has. When you're teaching someone music, he doesn't get music—he expresses the music that's already within him.

You and I don't have to go looking for faith. God has already placed the capacity to trust in and rely on him deep within every one of us. So, instead of seeking for more and more faith to help us feel better, we need to act on the small amount of faith we have, and then our faith will grow.

There is a truth here for all of us. Rock men don't have to sink. By faith they can walk on water. They can live the supernatural life.

As old-fashioned as it may seem, I am confident that the way out for Peter is the selfsame refuge for you and me. If we have come to a sense of defeat, if we are not getting anywhere in life, and if somehow the whole business of Christianity and life have been little better than a failure, we need not despair. There is a way out. We can turn to Christ, and he can lift us

FAITH: Rocks Don't Have to Sink

up. Try Peter's way. Apply the Saint Peter Principle. Take your gaze off your weakness and off the circumstances of life and fix it on Jesus Christ. Turn to Jesus and pray Peter's simple prayer, "Lord, save me." When you do that, you will find Jesus reaching out to lift you, not only out of your circumstances, but to your highest potential in character and career.

4
SELF-DENIAL
From Spirituality to Carnality

One of the hardest things to do is to die to self. Every time I try, Satan rushes in his emergency squad and gives me artificial respiration. He wants me to keep self alive and well, but death to self is a necessary part of the Saint Peter Principle. Like Peter, to reach one's highest potential in both character and career one must surrender his will to God's will. One must die to self.

Jesus taught us this in the experience known as "The Great Confession" (Matt. 16:13-18). When he and his disciples came to the region of Caesarea Philippi, Jesus asked them two key questions. The first was a leading question. A deeper and more penetrating one was to follow. He asked first, "Who do men say that I, the son of man, am?" This was not the question of an insecure leader seeking to know how he stood in the public polls. It was rather a probing question designed to determine the extent to which people were discovering the true nature of Jesus' mission and message. Jesus wanted to know the depths of their understanding of him.

Their answers were extremely complimentary. Jesus had been called some ugly names throughout his ministry. He had been called "gluttonous, and a winebibber," (Matt. 11:19), "a friend of publicans and sinners," (Matt. 27:63), and a blasphemer. But the disciples had bypassed all of these in their thinking. They told him that some people were calling him John the Baptist; some, Elijah; and others, Jeremiah or one of the prophets.

SELF-DENIAL: From Spirituality to Carnality

Seeing the growth of their understanding, Jesus now asked them a second question. It is the ultimate question of life: "Whom say ye that I am?" (Matt. 16:15). Why is this question so important? Because it determines not only who we think Jesus is but also what we are and what we do. The ideas men hold about industry, wealth, government, morals, and religion mold their society and alter their lives. What we think about Jesus is of even greater importance. It determines our relationship to God, our capacity for life, our character and our conduct, our capacity for love, our courage in the face of death, and where we will spend eternity. That's why it is life's ultimate question.

Peter, who by this time was emerging as the spokesman and leader of the disciples, responded, "Thou art the Christ, the Son of the living God" (Matt. 16:16). This answer was not the result of early enthusiasm but of divine revelation.

The disciples were really beginning to understand who Jesus was. Remember that the word *Christ* means Messiah. Peter was saying, "You are the anointed King of Israel; you are the fulfillment of all Old Testament prophecy; you are the embodiment of the hopes and dreams of the ages; you are God's chosen Son." What a truth! No wonder this has been called "The Great Confession."

Now that the disciples believed that Jesus was the Messiah, Jesus was then ready to explain the nature of his redemptive work, the true character of his messiahship. Then Jesus told them that he "must" go to Jerusalem, suffer many things, be killed, and then be raised again on the third day (see Matt. 16:21). That word *must* suggests deep conviction. Here was a man under orders. Here was a man on a mission. He was expressing what was God's will, God's way, and God's work for his life.

This was a shocking disclosure. This is not what they expected out of the Messiah. They shared the Jewish expectations that the Messiah would be a political deliverer who would defeat Rome, reestablish the kingdom of Israel, and usher in a period of peace and prosperity not known since the kingdom of David. They thought of the Messiah in terms of power and conquest, victory, and reign. But Jesus was talking about suffering and death. And they were not ready for that.

Peter in his characteristically presumptuous way took Jesus aside and chided him. He was not prepared to accept death for the Messiah. So, with a gesture implying superior knowledge, he suggested to Jesus that he should not follow through with this plan.

Then Jesus turned to Peter and said, "Get thee behind me, Satan: thou art an offense unto me: for thou savourest not the things that be of God, but those that be of men" (Matt. 16:23). This was a strong statement. Jesus branded Peter's protest as satanic. Why did Jesus use such strong language toward Peter? Because Peter was urging upon Jesus the very thing that the Satan was always whispering to Jesus. Satan was constantly suggesting to Jesus that there could be a crown without a cross, that there was another way to redeem the world other than by suffering and death. That posed a severe temptation to Jesus. It was the same temptation he had struggled with in the wilderness at the outset of his ministry. Now he found Satan coming to him again, this time trying to speak through Jesus' own followers.

Peter had become "an offense," a means of stumbling, to Christ. Peter had moved from a foundation stone to a stumbling stone, from the great confession to the great collapse, from a recipient of revelation to an instrument of insidious insinuation.

Do you know anything of that? Have you ever moved from the heights of spirituality one moment to the depths of carnality the next? I have. There have been times when I have preached like an angel, and then on my way home from church, acted like the devil. What a bundle of inconsistencies we all can be at times.

SELF-DENIAL: From Spirituality to Carnality

Jesus identified the source of Peter's problem when He said, "For thou savourest not the things that be of God, but those that be of men." The word *savourest* means "to think." Peter's problem was carnal thinking. He was not thinking as God thinks but as people think. How do humans think? They think basically of themselves. They put their own wishes, ambitions, desires, comforts, and safety first. They are selfish. In short, they look after old number one. And nobody had to write a book to teach them how.

This is not God's way. God's way is one of love, sacrifice, and unselfishness. He puts the well-being of others first, even if he must suffer to do it. God's way is the avenue of self-giving and surrender. It is the pathway of death to self.

Peter had decided to follow Jesus, but he had not given up his ambition for Jesus to become the king of Israel. Simon Peter still controlled Peter. He needed another lesson in discipleship, this time not in faith but in thinking. Just as his faith had been faulty in the previous chapter, so now his thinking was faulty. He needed to commit his thinking process to God—if Peter were ever to achieve his highest potential spiritually. He would have to die to self—to put his wishes, comforts, ambitions, and ease aside for the will of God. He would have to realize there can never be a crown without a cross, there could never be life without death, and there could never be redemption without crucifixion.

Death to self is the route to spiritual achievement. It is the way of discipleship, the way of deliverance, and the way of destiny. We somehow must learn to think this way, too, if we are to avoid a great collapse in our lives.

The Way of Discipleship

Death to self is the way to discipleship. Jesus seized this opportunity to teach Peter and all the disciples, "If any man will come after me, let him deny himself, and take up his cross, and follow me" (Matt. 16:24). He was saying, "The way of the cross and the way of sacrifice is not only the way for me, but it is the way for all of those who will be my disciples. You face the same choice between selfishness and selflessness that I face. As I have yielded my desires, ambitions, and will to God, so you must yield yourself to his will." The Master's way must become our way. His "must" must become our must.

We must deny ourselves. This is more than doing without something or giving up something. It is saying "no" to self instead of saying "no" to God. The basis of all sin is saying "no" to God. All sin is rooted in self-love, self-trust, self-assertion. To be Jesus' disciples, we must dethrone self and enthrone God. We must deny ourselves in order to affirm God and his will in our lives.

Then we must take up our cross. The cross is not some burden forced on us. It is something we voluntarily assume, something we take up because we want to. It represents God's will for our lives. Jesus' cross was different from ours. His was the cross of world redemption. Only he could carry that cross and atone for man's sins. But as the cross represented God's will for Jesus' life, so it represents God's will for our lives. We must take up whatever God wants us to do. The cross was a well-known instrument (and symbol) for suffering and death. All of those who heard Jesus that day understood what it meant, for they had seen hundreds of people die on crosses. To be his disciples, we must be willing to do the will of God at all costs.

Then we must follow after him. We must take up the same cause, walk the same path, and be willing to pay the same price. We must follow Jesus in character, conduct, and commitment.

Christ was devoid of self-centeredness. Instead of thinking of himself, he thought of God's will and man's need. He was willing to endure great suffering if the ultimate victory could be

SELF-DENIAL: From Spirituality to Carnality

achieved for God. His way must be our way. It is the way of utter denial and self-sacrifice.

We, too, must learn to think this way, for it is the way to discipleship.

The Way to Deliverance

Death to self is also the way of deliverance. Jesus went on to say, "For whosoever will save his life shall lose it: and whosoever will lose his life for my sake shall find it. For what is a man profited, if he shall gain the whole world, and lose his own soul? or what shall a man give in exchange for his soul?" (Matt. 16:25-26).

In these verses, Jesus tells us how we can be delivered from a life of emptiness, a life devoid of meaning. He is not playing with theory. He is talking about something we all want. To find real life is life's greatest prize. If you gain everything else in the world and fail to find a meaningful life, you have gained nothing. If you want to find a meaningful life, this is how to do it. You must die to yourself; you must lose yourself in the cause of God. This is not just good advice to be taken or ignored. This is unbreakable truth.

Life can't be found by seeking it. Many people spend all their energy in a never-ending pursuit of life. They try pleasure, sex, marriage, work, drugs, travel, social service, and even religion. They are always changing things, always between jobs, always between mates, always between careers, as if they will be able to find life out there somewhere. The end result is that they are fed up at fifteen and faded out at forty.

One of the biggest problems we face today is boredom. Every two minutes of every hour of every day, somebody attempts suicide in the United States. Every twenty minutes someone succeeds. Every day more than seventy-five people kill themselves in the most affluent society in history. Suicide is the tenth leading cause of death among all people and third leading cause of death among teenagers and college students.

What is the cause of suicide? It is emptiness and boredom! The cure for emptiness and boredom is a meaningful life. But where can we find that? A meaningful and happy life is a by-product of commitment . . . a commitment so deep and abiding that you are willing to die for it. The person who has nothing to die for has nothing to live for. It is as simple as that.

The choice is clear for all of us. It is self-love or self-loss. The conflict goes on in every one of us, and until we learn to put God's will above our own, we will never find deliverance from a meaningless life.

If you are tired of a meaningless life, boredom, and chasing empty rainbows, lose your life in Christ's cause, and you will find life at its best.

The Way of Destiny

Finally, death to self is the way to destiny. Jesus said, "For the son of man shall come in the glory of his Father with his angels; and then he shall reward every man according to his works" (Matt. 16:27).

These verses contain both a promise and a warning. There is the threefold promise that he will return, that he will reign, and that he will reward every man according to his works.

Then there is the warning of judgment. Judgment is inevitable. Life is going somewhere. It is going to the judgment seat of Christ. We shall all ultimately stand before him. It is only as we die to self that we shall share in his reign.

Jesus knew that out of crucifixion would come resurrection—out of death would come life. Everybody knows, according to David Redding, that death did something terrible to Christ, but not everyone knows that he did something wonderful to death. The great message of the New Testament is

SELF-DENIAL: From Spirituality to Carnality

not a tragic cry, "Help!" but a triumphant shout, "Hallelujah!"

When Jesus spoke of sacrifice, suffering, and crucifixion, Peter thought only of death, doom, and defeat. That's how we mortals think. He needed to learn that out of death was going to come life. Out of crucifixion would come resurrection. Out of ruin would come reign. That's God way! It is only as we share in his death that we shall share in this glorious destiny. So we must all die to self to become all God wants us to be.

It is the only way to discipleship, deliverance, and destiny. Spiritual achievement always requires this alteration of thought. Peter had to think "sacrifice" and not "self-preservation," and so must we. Once we are vulnerable to God's will, we become moldable clay in the Potter's hand.

5

INVOLVEMENT
From Inspiration to Perspiration

A man arrived at the church late. At the door he asked the usher, "Is the service over?" "No," replied the usher, "worship is over, but the service is just beginning." Some people mistakenly equate the two, but there is a vast difference between worship, and service, between inspiration and perspiration. If we are ever to achieve our highest spiritual potential, we must learn the difference between them and keep them in balance in our lives.

Learning this lesson was a logical step in Peter's spiritual progress. Jesus had prophesied great things for Peter and had called him to a monumental work. But it would take a long time to bring his character and career to their full potential. He would have to learn to trust in Jesus and not in his own strength. And he would have to learn to think as God thinks and not as humans think.

Now he was prepared for his next lesson. He also had to learn to keep a balance in his life between worship and work.

Jesus taught him this balance in the experience known as the "transfiguration" (Matt. 17:1-9). In the previous chapter, Jesus had confronted the disciples with two questions concerning his identity. He had asked, "Whom do men say that I the Son of man am?" and "Whom say ye that I am?" (Matt. 16:13,15). These were carefully designed questions to discover the depth of their understanding as to who he really was. Peter answered the last question correctly when he said, "Thou art the Christ, the Son of the living God."

INVOLVEMENT: From Inspiration to Perspiration

Now that the disciples were beginning to understand who he was, they were ready to understand the nature of his messiahship. So Jesus told them of his coming crucifixion.

This was so contrary to their concept of the Messiah that Peter tried to persuade Jesus that there was surely another way to redeem his people. Jesus insisted that he *must* suffer and die in order to redeem the world. Moreover, he said that all who became his disciples must be willing to do the same thing. They too must be willing to deny themselves, take up their crosses, and follow after him. The ideas of crucifixion and resurrection were so contrary to the popular ideas of the Messiah that it would take a while for them to accept it. So Jesus let these truths soak into their minds for a few days.

But Jesus knew that if the disciples were to face the troublesome days in the future, they would need further confirmation that he was the divine Son of God. They had confessed it. Now it needed to be confirmed in such a way that nothing could ever make them doubt it again. The great confession would need to become a steel-like conviction.

It is easy to walk through the sunshine and even the showers of life with a soft faith. But when the storms of life are raging, your faith had better be solid. It is easy to pray "Thy will be done" while you sit on soft cushions in an air-conditioned cathedral. It is not so easy when you stand at the bedside of a dying child. In the shattering experiences of life, we must be sure of ourselves and sure of him.

God's Confirmation

Six days later, Jesus took three of his disciples onto a mountain to confirm the great confession. He chose Peter, James, and John because they probably were closest to him in understanding and sympathy. There were three marvelous acts in this drama on the mountain.

First, Jesus was transfigured before them. As he prayed, his face began to shine with the brightness of the sun, and his clothing turned to a dazzling white. He literally took on the glow of heaven itself. Jesus, the Son of God, usually wore homespun garb and looked like an ordinary Galilean peasant. As he prayed on the mountain that day, his Deity shone through, and the disciples beheld that he was the Son of God. This transfiguration was a confirmation of the great confession.

Then Moses and Elijah appeared with Jesus and talked with him about his coming death. There is deep significance in those two men being with Jesus. They were perhaps the two greatest men in the Old Testament. Moses was the lawgiver. Elijah was representative of all the prophets. In them, all of history rose up to confirm Jesus as the Son of God. Their presence and conversation meant that they were adding their testimony to his mission as Messiah. He was the one of whom they had dreamed, hoped, and foretold. They were giving assent to his Deity and his death. They, too, were confirming the great confession.

Surely this was confirmation enough for anyone. But there was still one more act to follow. Not only did the lawgiver and prophet affirm his Deity, now the voice of God spoke: "This is my beloved Son, in whom I am well pleased; hear ye him" (Matt. 17:5).

The purpose of this experience was to confirm the three apostles' faith. It etched itself indelibly into the minds of the apostles. Peter never forgot it. Years later, he wrote that he and the apostles were not following mere tales about Jesus, but that they were eyewitnesses to Christ's majesty and glory. Then he told about this experience on the mount of transfiguration where he saw the glory of Jesus with his own eyes and heard the voice of God with his own ears (2 Peter 1:16-18). This was proof enough for him that Jesus was the Christ, the Son of the living God.

INVOLVEMENT: From Inspiration to Perspiration

As all of this happened, the disciples were so awestruck that they fell on their faces in fright. Then Jesus came to them, touched them, and told them not to be afraid. When they lifted up their eyes, they saw no one but Jesus—"Jesus only."

Then they were to go to Jerusalem. As they left the mountain and journeyed back to the valley below, Jesus kept charging them that they should tell no man about this until He was resurrected from the dead. This experience was not for publication but for confirmation. It was not for preaching; it was for preparation for the future.

It was a marvelous experience except for one dark spot. That was Peter's initial response when he saw Jesus transfigured with Moses and Elijah by his side. Matthew tells us that Peter was so shaken that he did not know what to say. But, in typical Petrine fashion, he said something anyhow. He said, "Lord, it is good for us to be here: if thou wilt, let us make here three tabernacles; one for thee, and one for Moses, and one for Elias" (Matt. 17:4).

Peter had nothing to say, and he said it! Lincoln once commented that it is "better to remain silent and be thought a fool than to open your mouth and remove all doubt." Peter in his impulsiveness never left any doubt.

He was so caught up, so thrilled, with this experience of inspiration that he wanted to stay on the mountaintop. He did not want to go back down to the valley where there was suffering, heartache, and misery. He did not want to go on to Jerusalem where death awaited his Master. He wanted to remain there in isolation and in inspiration. The word *good* means "beautiful, excellent, pleasing." Peter loved this experience and wanted to prolong it as long as possible. He, in fact, was content to let the experience be an end within itself. He was willing to forget about the conflicts, crises, and the crucifixion which lay ahead. He thought, "Wouldn't it be better to remain on the mountain in heavenly fellowship?"

This suggestion was so absurd that Jesus didn't even answer him. Never was silence more eloquent than at this moment. Peter had missed the whole purpose of the moment of inspiration. It was to prepare him and the other disciples for the valley below. It was to strengthen and solidify their faith for the future. At that very moment in the valley below, the other disciples were struggling with suffering, heartache, and failure. A distraught father had brought his epileptic boy to them to be healed. They had tried and failed. In the valley below, there was disease, despair, distress, and discouragement. Jesus and his disciples were needed below. The mountaintop was to prepare them for just such experiences. The mountain of inspiration was not intended for isolation, but to prepare them for ministry in the valley.

The evidence? Jesus went straight from the mountain of transformation to the valley of tribulation. He went from the awe of God's glory to the agony of man's suffering. He left the voice of God to answer the voice of men.

The Balance We Need

This is always God's way. The balance of the Christian life is to meet God in the holy place and then to minister to man in the marketplace.

This was a lesson Peter needed to learn. He needed to learn the balance between inspiration and perspiration, between worship and work. It was another step in his becoming.

We must learn this, too. It is so easy to become lopsided in our faith. One of the dangers of the "deeper-life" movement is that we can become content with inspiration only, that we will spend so much time going to conferences, attending conventions, listening to tapes, reading books, participating in Bible studies, and deepening our own spiritual lives that we fail to mix in the valley of human suffering. There is the danger that we shall so enjoy the fellowship of our church and of our Christian friends that we never reach out in ministry to those who are sick in sin.

The mountaintop is important, but it is never an end within itself. We must move quickly from the mountain of inspiration to the valley of service. What is the purpose of inspiration? It is for preparation, penetration, and perspiration.

Inspiration Is for Preparation

We must have time alone with God. This is the time of preparation, when our faith is confirmed, verified, and strengthened. It is a period when we are edified, built up spiritually. But it is never an end within itself. It is always preparing us for a greater ministry for our Lord and for humanity.

Isaiah, the prophet, said, "They that wait upon the Lord shall renew their strength; they shall mount up with wings as eagles; they shall run, and not be weary; and they shall walk, and not faint" (Isa. 40:31). We are told to wait on the Lord. But to what purpose? Why wait on the Lord? Why study the Bible? Why pray? Why worship? Why go on retreats? Why attend conferences?—that we might be renewed in our strength, that we might mount up with wings as eagles, that we might run and not be weary, that we might walk and not faint. The purpose of waiting is that we may be renewed for work. The purpose of inspiration is preparation.

One of the titanic failures of most Christians is that we have not learned to wait on the Lord. We are people of action. We say we would rather "wear out than rust out." We may know how to witness, and we know how to work. But we do not know how to wait on the Lord. That's the reason we do not soar to spiritual heights. That's the reason we grow so weary in our Christian struggle. That's the reason so many faint and fall out in walking after the Lord. We have not waited, and, therefore, we have not been renewed.

If you think we know how to wait on the Lord, look around in the average worship service on Sunday morning. If the preacher goes a minute past twelve, you will see more wiggling than waiting. We can't wait on the Lord for worrying that we might have to wait in the cafeteria line. We can't wait on the Lord; we've got to get home and see the Bucks play the Goats.

That's why our Christianity is so often weighted instead of winged. That's why the wonder of it soon turns to a weariness. That's why so many fall out of the race long before the finish. We must learn to wait on God in prayer, Bible study, and worship. Without inspiration, there is no preparation for service and ministry.

Inspiration Is for Penetration

Inspiration is never intended as an end in itself. It is never for isolation. It is meant to prepare us to penetrate the valleys of strife and suffering, failure and sorrow, death and despair. We must have inspiration. We must draw near to God and feel his presence, but we must not stop there and bask in the glory of his presence. The mountaintop is always more enjoyable than the valley. The daily struggle of the way of the cross is always more difficult than the retreat or the conference time. But these moments of inspiration are to prepare us to get involved in ministering to our world.

George McLeod put it this way:

> I simply argue that the cross be raised again
>   at the center of the marketplace
>   as well as on the steeple of the church.
> I am rediscovering the claim that
>   Jesus was not crucified in a cathedral
>   between two candles

INVOLVEMENT: From Inspiration to Perspiration

> but on a cross between two thieves;
> on the town garbage heap,
> at a crossroad so cosmopolitan
> that they had to write His title
> in Latin and in Hebrew and in Greek.
> At the kind of place where cynics talk smut
> and thieves curse and soldiers gamble;
> Because that is where He died
> and that is what He died about
> and that is where Christians ought to be
> and what Christians ought to be about.[1]

That's the way Jesus wants it. He prayed for the disciples and for us, "I pray not that thou shouldest take them out of the world, but that thou shouldest keep them from the evil. They are not of the world, even as I am not of the world" (John 17:15-16). Jesus wants us "in" the world but not "of" the world. What does it mean for a Christian to be in the world? It does not mean to be like the world; the marks of a Christian are to make us different. Nor does it mean we are to abandon Christian fellowship. It means we are to know non-Christians, befriend them, and enter into their lives to the extent that we influence them with the gospel, rather than their infecting us with their worldiness.

We are to be as Christ was in the world. We are sent into the world by him as he was sent into the world by the Father. We are to be in our mission as Jesus was in his mission. We are to be like the One we are presenting to the world.

We may be producing a new generation of monks, sitting in their evangelical sanctuaries and praying for God to do the work in the world that he intended them to do. We must ever guard against that.

What's the use of pulling your car into a filling station and getting a tank of gas if you don't intend to run the car? The purpose of filling is running.

Someone has said, "Every person should have three conversions. A man needs to be converted to Jesus Christ: 'Believe on the Lord Jesus Christ, and thou shalt be saved, and thy house' (Acts 16:31); to the church: 'not forsaking the assembling of ourselves together' (Heb. 10:25); and finally converted back to the world: 'Go ye into all the world, and preach the gospel to every creature' (Mark 16:15)."

Have you experienced these three conversions? We will never achieve our highest spiritual potential until we are penetrating our world for Jesus Christ.

Inspiration Is for Perspiration

It is not enough to meet God on the mountain or to mix with people along the trail; we must move on to minister to the multitudes. We must roll up our sleeves and enter into the struggles of people through ministry. The purpose of inspiration is also the perspiration of hard work.

We are not saved to sit, soak, and sour, or even to survey the situation. We are saved to serve.

In his new autobiography, *Adventures of a Bystander*, management consultant Peter Drucker contends, "The greatest sin . . . may be the new, the twentieth-century sin of indifference, the sin of the distinguished biochemist-physiologist who neither kills nor lies but refuses to bear witness when, in the words of the old gospel hymn, 'They Crucified My Lord.' "[2]

George Bernard Shaw hammers home the same nail in *The Devil's Disciple*. Judith says, "Oh, I know it's wrong to hate anybody, but. . . ." Anderson replies, "Oh, come, dear, you're not so wicked as you think. The worst sin toward our fellow creatures is not to hate them, but to be indifferent to them. That's the essence of inhumanity."[3]

Indifference will stifle and strangle our spiritual achievement. It is in the valley of perspiration that God often does his greatest work. I have aspirations to be a writer. Occasionally when I see a beautiful mountain lodge or a lakeside cabin, I think, "What a book I could write here!" The quiet, serenity, and peacefulness of it appeals to me. Then I remember that the apostle Paul wrote many of his letters, not from a penthouse but from a prison. Amid the sweat, swearing, suffering, and stench of life, God did his greatest work.

If we are ever going to achieve our potential, we must leave the isolation ward called the church and enter the emergency room of human suffering. We must meet people where they are bruised and broken by sin and suffering and minister to them in the name of Jesus. The mountain of inspiration is vital. But its purpose is preparation, penetration, and perspiration.

And all of these must have their proper place in our life if we are to reach full spiritual maturity.

Notes

1. George McCleod, *Living Quotations for Christians,* comp. and ed. Sherwood Eliot Wirt and Kersten Beckstrom (New York: Harper & Row Publishers, 1974), p. 44.

2. Peter Drucker, *Adventures of a Bystander* (New York: Harper & Row, 1979), p. 169.

3. George Bernard Shaw, *Nine Plays* (New York: Dodd Mead, 1948), p. 300.

6

RECONCILIATION
Receiving and Giving Forgiveness

Former President Gerald Ford, in his book *A Time To Heal,* focused on the confusing and tragic twilight of the Nixon presidency. Clearly, Nixon was guilty of a cover-up in the Watergate case, but he refused to admit it. His pride kept him from doing so. If he had been willing to confess his guilt and ask the American people for forgiveness, he would probably have received it.

President Ford then faced a grievous dilemma. Should he let the legal charges run their course and allow Nixon to be indicted and tried? Or should he pardon him? If he decided on justice, the process would probably have taken years and would have blotted out everything else in the country until it was over. He therefore decided to pardon the former president, feeling it was best for the nation.

He explained his decision: "America needed recovery, not revenge. The hate had to be drained and the healing begun."[1]

There are times when all of us face the same choice. Will we seek revenge, or will we seek recovery? Will we demand justice or mercy? Will we condemn, or will we pardon? Others hurt us, wrong us, and offend us. They lie about us, abuse us, and mistreat us.

When this happens, the natural tendency is to become resentful, bitter, and vengeful. The world is full of broken relationships, wounded spirits, and unresolved quarrels. There are multitudes of people who have been hurt and have never

RECONCILIATION: Receiving and Giving Forgiveness 61

forgiven the person who hurt them. Their lives are filled with hatred and unforgivingness.

Hatred is one of the most destructive forces in life. It is like a cancer in the soul. Of all the emotions that tear the personality into shreds, there is none equal to hate. It is a poison to the body, to the mind and to the soul. It is dangerous, not only because of what it might cause us to do to others but also because of what it does to us. It consumes our time, our thoughts, and our energy. It destroys us physically, emotionally, and spiritually. Shakespeare wrote: "Heat not the furnace so hot that you singe yourself." Vengeance, the offspring of hatred, is a cancer which, if left unchecked, consumes both the possessor and his foe. And someone has said, "For every minute of hating, you lose sixty seconds of happiness."

So, it is imperative then that we learn to forgive those who wrong us. In dealing with others, we need to major on recovery, not on revenge.

This was a lesson that Simon Peter had to learn in his journey of discipleship. If he was ever to achieve his highest spiritual potential, he had to learn to forgive other people.

Jesus taught him this in response to the question, "Lord, how often shall my brother sin against me, and I forgive him? Till seven times?" (Matt. 18:21). This was not an impulsive question. It grew out of Jesus' teachings about how to deal with the wrongs other people do us.

Jesus gave us a careful, step-by-step plan for dealing with those who offend us (Matt. 18:15-20). He began by stating that the offended person is to take the initiative in seeking reconciliation. The wisdom of this is obvious. Some people have gone on for years nursing grudges against people who didn't even know they were being accused, much less what they were being accused of. Often only the person who has been hurt is in the position to take the initiative.

Also, if the innocent person sits back and waits for the guilty person to apologize, the grievance will probably never be resolved. The reason is that we seldom think we are wrong. We usually believe the problem rests in the other person. Pride enters the picture, and we find it difficult to admit that we are wrong. So, we must always take the initiative.

Then, he gives us his progressive plan on how to deal with offenses. First, you should take your grievance to the person privately and prayerfully, without waiting for an apology. This is the first step love makes in dealing with a delicate issue. If that doesn't work, then you should take a group of two or three objective friends and let them serve as mediators. If that doesn't work, the matter should be taken before the church. If that doesn't succeed, the matter is still not to be dropped. It is to be carried ultimately to heaven in a concert of prayer. It is in this context that Jesus said, "If two of you shall agree on earth as touching any thing that they shall ask, it shall be done for them of my Father which is in heaven" (Matt. 18:19). From the Greek word for *agree* we get our English word *symphony.* It describes a group of instruments playing in harmony with one another. There is massive power in the symphonic prayers of God's people. We should not stop short of heaven in dealing with our grievances with other people.

This plan was designed to help us grapple with personal differences in a positive and constructive manner. Its intent is to help us transform our enemies into brothers. After all, there are two ways to get rid of an enemy. You can kill him, or you can make a friend of him. Jesus taught us the latter . . . the way of recovery, not of revenge.

How Often Is Enough?

It is out of this background that Peter asked, "Lord, how oft shall my brother sin against me, and I forgive him? till seven times?" (Matt. 18:21). No doubt, Peter thought he was being

RECONCILIATION: Receiving and Giving Forgiveness

unusually generous. After all, the Jewish law only required that you forgive a man three times. After that many offenses, you were free to treat him as an enemy. Peter was going far beyond the requirements of the Jewish law.

Jesus could see that Peter had failed to comprehend the true nature of forgiveness. So he told him that he should not stop at forgiving a person seven times, but should keep on forgiving until seventy times seven. He should show unlimited and unending forgiveness. Forgiveness is a matter of attitude, not arithmetic. It is not a matter of calculations in the head but of compassion in the heart.

To illustrate this truth, Jesus told the parable of the unforgiving servant. A king had a servant who owed him ten thousand talents. That was an enormous sum of money. It would amount to several million dollars in our day. It was more than any person listening to Jesus could ever pay in his lifetime. The king demanded that the debt be paid. When the servant could not do so, the king threatened to have his wife and children sold into slavery. So the servant fell on his knees before the king and begged for mercy. The king took pity on him and completely forgave him the debt.

This forgiven servant then went to a man who owed him a hundred pence—a very small sum of money. He literally grabbed the man by the throat and demanded payment of the debt. The man couldn't pay, and so the servant had him thrown into prison.

When the king heard about this, he said, "You wicked servant. I forgave you all the debt, because you asked me; shouldn't you have had compassion on your fellow servant, even as I had pity on you?" And the angry lord delivered him to the jailers, until he should pay all his debt. Then Jesus said, "So likewise shall my heavenly father do also unto you, if you from your hearts do not forgive your brothers their trespasses." (See Matt. 18:23-35.)

What Is Forgiveness?

The word *forgive* literally means "to send away, to let off." An unforgiving spirit, bitterness, and resentment build invisible barriers among people. They divide people. To forgive means that we no longer allow those feelings to come between us. When we forgive another person, the barriers that divide us are removed and the relationship is restored.

Real forgiveness is genuine and heartfelt. It is not superficial. It is not merely thin veneer. It is so easy to develop a false front, an onionskin facade. That is hypocrisy. Jesus is not talking about improving our acting ability. Most of us are capable of academy-award performances when it comes to acting nice to people we don't like. We can smile sweetly and shake their hands outwardly while we inwardly seethe with resentment toward them. Jesus is talking about forgiveness that flows from the heart.

If we ever reach our full spiritual capability, we need to practice unlimited forgiveness, as Jesus taught us here. It is an essential ingredient to discipleship . . . to becoming all that we are capable of being in both character and career. We dare not carry around unresolved quarrels and grievances. To do so is like carrying around a bag of stones. As the bag slowly fills, it impedes our progress in the Christian life. So we must learn the lesson of unlimited and unending forgiveness. The price of forgiveness is often high, but the price of alienation is higher. Forgiveness is not a luxury. It is a necessity.

God Forgave You, Didn't He?

Jesus gives us two reasons why we must be forgiving. *First, because of our experience.* We have been freely forgiven, therefore we must freely forgive. The question of the king in the parable is a probing one. "I forgave you all of your debts,

RECONCILIATION: Receiving and Giving Forgiveness

because you asked me. Shouldn't you also have had compassion on your fellow servant, even as I had compassion on you?"

The simple fact is that God has forgiven us; therefore, we ought to forgive others. The forgiveness of God is not just to be rejoiced in. It is to be duplicated. The grace of God should inspire us to be gracious. Forgiveness ought to inspire forgiveness.

Stuart Briscoe expressed the thought when he wrote: "In your experience of the forgiveness of God, learn to forgive the boss who abused your willing spirit, the church that failed to meet your expectations, the spouse who hurt you, and the kids who disgraced you. God forgave you, didn't he?"

The parable of the unmerciful servant illustrates how God deals with us. He was hopelessly and helplessly in debt. Debt is a common figure in the New Testament for sin. Jesus is always seeking to help us recognize the helplessness of our position before God. We are in debt to him, and there is no way to pay him back or buy him off. We are bankrupt. If we were brought into his presence, none of us could stand on his own two feet. The debt we owe to God is so enormous no one can pay it. We are hopelessly insolvent.

The psalmist said, "If thou, Lord, shouldest mark iniquities, O Lord, who shall stand?" (Ps. 130:3). The word *mark* is a bookkeeping term. It means to enter into a ledger. If God should enter into the ledger book of eternity all of our sins, strike a line at the bottom and total them up and demand full payment, none of us could stand in his presence. We are God's debtors, and we have nothing with which to pay. Our only hope is his mercy and forgiveness. And it has been given to us through the Lord Jesus Christ. Now that we have received it, we should share it.

Here is a warning against living a double life—receiving and not giving, accepting mercy and demanding justice, desiring to be treated tenderly and then acting harshly. A Christian has no right to lay aside all traces of his inward experience with God when it comes to dealing with other people. We must at least show signs of our experience of grace through our relationships. We dare not go out from the mercy of God onto the hard streets of life with an unforgiving heart.

If we find it hard to forgive and if, like Peter to whom this parable was spoken, we find that we can forgive seven times and no more, then let us go back to the place where we made our reckoning with God—to the cross of Jesus Christ, see grace again, and remember our experiences and our needs. Remember that we joined the world in driving nails into his hands and feet and while we did it, he prayed, "Father, forgive them; for they know not what they do" (Luke 23:34). The forgiveness we have experienced from God we should now express to others.

Will You Sin Again?

Second, we must forgive not only because of our past experience, but also because of our present and future need. Jesus spoke strong words when he said, "So likewise shall my heavenly Father do also unto you, if ye from your hearts forgive not every one his brother their trespasses" (Matt. 18:35).

The truth is as simple as this. Unless you plan on not sinning again, you had best not quit forgiving. Unless you intend to quit asking for forgiveness after seven times, don't quit giving forgiveness after seven times.

There is a close parallel between our forgiveness of others and God's forgiveness of us. We must get the horizontal relationships of life right because they affect the vertical relationship. We cannot be right with God and wrong with man at the same time.

The Conditions for Forgiveness

The Scriptures set out at least three conditions for our forgiveness. They are conversion, confession, and compassion. Look at them for a moment.

First, there is conversion. Peter says, "Repent ye therefore, and be converted, that your sins may be blotted out" (Acts 3:19). The word *blot* is also a bookkeeping term. It means to erase from the ledger books. It came from a time when ink had no acid in it and therefore did not bite into the paper. It just lay on the top of the page and dried. Paper was very valuable and was therefore used again and again. So, if a writer made a mistake in writing or was through with a piece of parchment he had used before, he would not wad it up and throw it away. He would take a wet sponge and wipe it across the dried ink. This would soften the ink and it could be wiped away leaving no trace. That's what God does with our sins when we are converted. He blots them out. What we need is not to turn over a new leaf on top of the old leaves in life. We need the old leaves wiped clean. When we repent and are converted, God does this for us.

Second, confession. John writes, "If we confess our sins, he is faithful and just to forgive us our sins, and to cleanse us of all unrighteousness" (1 John 1:9). Someone has called this their soap bar verse. It tells us how we can have spiritual cleansing. The word *confess* means "to agree with." It means "to say the same thing as." God has repeatedly accused us of sin both in the Scriptures and in our consciences. When we confess our sins, we are simply agreeing with God. We are saying, "Father, what you have said about me in the Bible and in my own heart is exactly right. I am a sinner. I have transgressed your laws. I have done wrong." That kind of confession to God brings cleansing from sin.

The third condition is compassion. We must be compassionate with others if we want God's compassion. We must forgive other people if we want God to forgive us. The Scriptures say, "Blessed are the merciful, for they shall receive mercy" (Matt. 5:7, NASB). In the Lord's Prayer Jesus taught us to pray, "Forgive us our debts, as we forgive our debtors" (Matt. 6:12). This is the only part of the Lord's Prayer he amplified upon. He closed out the prayer by saying that if we do not forgive other people of the wrongs they do to us, neither will our Heavenly Father forgive us of our sins.

When General Oglethorpe said to John Wesley, "I never forgive," Wesley properly answered, "Then I hope, sir, you never sin. For with what measure you mete, it shall be measured to you again."

Forgiveness is not ours on an exchange basis. The fact is that when we refuse to forgive other people, that spirit blocks the flow of God's grace into our lives. It clogs the channel. It creates a spiritual interference so the reception of forgiveness and grace is not possible. A man who does not forgive destroys the bridge over which he himself must travel. We shall have judgment without mercy if we show no mercy (Jas. 2:13). Divine and human forgiveness go hand in hand.

Someone has suggested that we need to make Ephesians 4:26 our evening prayer and Matthew 6:12 our morning prayer. Ephesians 4:26 says, "Be ye angry, and sin not: let not the sun go down upon your wrath." Matthew 6:12 says, "Forgive us our debts, as we forgive our debtors." If we can go to bed at night with all of our differences and grievances resolved, we will sleep better. Then we can get up in the morning praying that God will forgive us as we have forgiven others.

Jesus told us that there was a chance for the publicans, the harlots, and even for the Pharisees to enter the kingdom of God, but declared frankly that there is no chance for the unforgiving. We cannot be forgiven and be unforgiving. There is no settlement with God unless we settle with our fellow man.

Forgiveness Is Never Easy

Several weeks after I spoke on this subject in my church, one of our deacons sought me out, telling me the effect the message had on his life. He testified that for twenty years he and a man he worked with had not spoken to each other except when necessary. Years before, they had undergone a disagreement that had left a deep cleavage in their relationship. After hearing this message, that deacon went to the man, apologized, and asked if they could be friends. The man refused, saying that his hurt was too deep to forgive. My deacon friend told that fellow he must deal with his own feelings, but that, as for his part, there were no more hard feelings. He was giving and asking forgiveness. The deacon said it was as if a heavy weight and burden had been lifted from his shoulders, and he experienced a joy that he had not known in twenty years.

This kind of action is never easy. As C. S. Lewis said, "Everyone says forgiveness is a lovely idea, until he has something to forgive." It is doubly hard when the offender does not repent. But we must learn to do it anyhow. Forgiveness does not depend upon the character of the offender but upon the character of the *offended*. It does not come because of his worthiness but because of your love. It flows out of a heart of love, gratitude, humility, and brotherhood.

But if we aren't careful we will find an excuse not to do it. We will say, "I know I ought to forgive, but . . ." And before you know it you will have "butted" yourself clear out of a right relationship with God.

Forgiveness is an essential part of the Saint Peter Principle.

Without it, we stifle our own spiritual development. We hinder our own growth potential.

Like Peter, we have received forgiveness, and we need forgiveness. Therefore, we must give it freely if we are to continue moving toward being all we are intended to be.

Note

1. Gerald R. Ford, *A Time to Heal* (New York: Harper and Row, 1979), p. 161. Used by permission.

7
INFLUENCE
An Offense to None

There is an old story of a blind man who carried a lighted lantern at night. Someone asked him why he always went around at night with a lighted lantern since he could not see. He replied, "To keep others from stumbling over me." It wasn't a bad idea. He never stumbled over anyone else, at least not intentionally. But he didn't want anyone to stumble over him either.

That must be the concern of every true disciple. We must see to it that no one stumbles along the way because of us. Discipleship demands that kind of discipline.

Jesus taught Peter this lesson in one of the most unusual and unnoticed stories in the New Testament (Matt. 17:24-27). Jesus and his disciples had just returned to the city of Capernaum. His entrance to the town was not unnoticed by his enemies. They were alert to his every move. They watched him constantly. Presently the local tax collector, prompted no doubt by these enemies, asked Peter, "Doesn't your master pay taxes?" The negative form of the question suggests criticism. It was asked with malicious intent. He wanted to find some occasion to discredit Jesus.

The tax referred to here was a Temple tax. It was a small kind of "poll tax" expected of every Jewish man, rich or poor, above twenty years of age. Its purpose was to support Temple worship. The tax had its beginning in the days of Moses to support the tabernacle (Ex. 30:11-16), but by this time it had been transferred to support the Temple worship.

Worship was expensive in that day as it is in ours. The Temple at Jerusalem was costly to maintain. It took money to pay the worship leaders and provide sacrificial animals, inspectors of sacrifices, custodial services, priestly garments, and repairs on the building. While this tax was not compulsory, it was expected that every Jewish man would meet the obligation cheerfully.

Peter responded to the tax collector's question with an instant and confident "Yes." That's what you would expect from the impulsive Peter. He would answer for Jesus without bothering to ask him. However, he knew by general principle that whatever was right in such matters Jesus would do.

Later, when Peter went into the house, Jesus anticipated the whole encounter and said, "Simon, I want to know what you think about something. Do earthly kings collect taxes from their own children or from the citizens of their country?"

The answer was obvious. Kings do not tax their own household. In fact, it is for their household that they tax other people. The king's son pays no taxes. Peter knew that, and he answered it just that way. Jesus used this simple parable to remind Peter of something he already knew and to teach him something he needed yet to learn.

He was reminding Peter, "I am the Son of God. You confessed that at Caesarea Philippi. Then God confirmed it on the mountain of transfiguration. But now you seem to have forgotten it. If I am the Son of God, then I am not under obligation to support my Father's house. The Son of God does not have to pay taxes for the house of his Father."

Then Jesus said, "Nevertheless, lest anyone should be offended at me, we will pay the tax." The word *offend* means "to cause to stumble" or "to trip up." Jesus was saying, "Though I am under no obligation to do so, I will pay the tax lest I set a bad example for other people. I will not do anything

INFLUENCE: An Offense to None

that will be a bad influence on others." So he told Peter to go down to the sea, to cast a hook into the water and to catch a fish. He would find a coin that he was to use to pay their taxes in the mouth of the fish.

Jesus performed this miracle not because he needed the money. The tax was so small he could easily have had the amount. He performed the miracle to reaffirm the fact that he was the Son of God. Peter needed to be reminded of that in a vivid way. But he also needed to learn the place of influence in discipleship. If he was ever going to achieve his highest spiritual potential, he would have to strive never to be a stumbling block to anyone. He needed to learn one of the basic requirements of discipleship—to relinquish personal rights in the interest of others. This was Christ's way, and it must be the way of all of his disciples.

In this encounter when Jesus first spoke to Peter, he used his old name "Simon" that referred back to his beginning days of immaturity. For Peter was forgetting again that Jesus was the Son of God, that as his disciple, he still had a lot of developing to do.

Peter needed to be reminded that Jesus was the Son of God, and he needed to learn the ways of God. If he were ever to achieve his highest spiritual potential, he too would have to learn to live by this principle. It is the way of God to avoid causing anyone to stumble and fall spiritually.

Jesus would do nothing, would allow nothing that would hurt another, mislead another, or trip another. Here was a principle Peter needed to learn. People are always watching us. By what they see we become either a stepping-stone or a stumbling block to them. And we should not use our privileges or freedom as the sons of God in such a way as to cause anyone to stumble away from God. Even if we have to give up our personal rights to do so, we must seek to live inoffensive lives. We must learn the importance of influence and the principle of relinquishing personal rights where it can serve the interests of others.

The point is that Jesus did what he had a right not to do. He paid the Temple tax from which as he explained he was rightfully exempt. As Christians we should be willing to do the same. And the opposite is also true. We should be willing to give up what we might enjoy and what would be harmless to us if in any way it causes us to become a stumbling block to another.

Watch Out—They're Watching

As people were constantly watching Jesus, alert to his every move, scrutinizing his every activity, so they are always watching us. There is no way we can avoid it. None of us can escape it. Christians have a fishbowl existence.

This truth came to me with a fresh impact several months ago when I accompanied a group of Christian men on a fishing trip to Mexico. On our second day out, the fishing was a little slow, and so my partner asked our Mexican guide for a drink. The guide opened the ice chest, took out a soft drink, and said with a smile, "You are *hallelujahs.*" That was his way of identifying us as Christians. My friend replied, "Yes, how did you know?" The guide replied, "There is no beer in the icebox."

That experience lodged in my mind. People are always looking in the ice chests, magazine racks, the bookshelves, and other areas of our lives, and from what they see they are making judgments about us. What they see in those places gives them a hint of what is in our hearts. If someone unexpectedly looked into your ice chest, would they ever guess that you are a *hallelujah?* Like it or not, people are looking at you.

We have only four contacts with the world, you and I. We

INFLUENCE: An Offense to None

are evaluated and classified by these four things: (1) what we do, (2) how we look, (3) what we say, (4) how we say it. These are our means of communicating to the world—what we believe and what we are.

Paul describes the Corinthian Christians as "epistles, known and read of all men." He called them letters of Christ written not with pen and ink but with the spirit of the living God. And they were written not on tablets of stone but in flesh and blood (2 Cor. 3:2-3). The kind of letters he was talking about were letters of reference or recommendation. He was saying that every Christian is a letter of reference or recommendation for Jesus Christ.

Quite often I am asked to write a letter of reference or recommendation for someone. The inquirer usually wants to know things such as "How long have you known this person? What is your relationship to him? Is he honest? Dependable? Trustworthy?" By these letters of reference from me and from others, the inquirer forms a good or bad opinion concerning the person.

Every Christian is a letter of reference or recommendation for Christ. Whether we like it or not, our life is an advertisement for him. People judge him by what they see written in our lives and in our conduct. The world judges a shopkeeper by what he sells, a craftsman by the work he produces, a church by its members, and Christ by his followers.

Paul Gilbert expressed this truth when he wrote,

> You're writing a gospel,
> A chapter each day,
> By deeds that you do,
> And words that you say.
>
> Men read what you write,
> Whether faithful or true;
> Just what is the Gospel
> According to you?[1]

An Awesome Responsibility

The greatest handicap that Christ has is the unsatisfactory lives of professing Christians. As we go out into the world, we have the awe-inspiring responsibility of being open letters or advertisements for Christ and for his church. People are reading us, and by what we do and what we say we become either stumbling blocks or stepping-stones. This is an awesome fact.

Several years ago, a group of people from our church were in Belize Central America on a medical missions trip. They were working in the little town of Punta Gorda. One evening after their day of ministry, they were walking down the street when a lady selling lottery tickets came up and tried to sell them some lottery tickets. The leader of the group replied, "No! No! These people are Christians." With that, the lady turned and walked away without saying a word. Later, Dr. Marietta Walker said to me, "It's a funny feeling to see the high expectations these people have of Christians." The fact that they were Christians convinced the lady that there was no possibility of a sale, and so she turned and walked away in silence.

The world does have high expectations of us. It is an awesome responsibility to be a Christian.

Jesus once used a child as an object lesson to teach us the importance of influence. He placed the child on his knee and then reminded us that in the world it is inevitable that there will be stumbling blocks to cause people to sin. But he said, "Pity the person who causes another person to stumble and fall. It would be better for that person to have a millstone tied around his neck and his body cast into the sea than that he should ever trip up another person" (Matt. 18:6-9, author's paraphrase).

Tying a millstone around a person's neck and casting him into the sea was an ancient form of capital punishment. Na-

INFLUENCE: An Offense to None

tions have always had means of dealing with capital offenses. In our country we use the electric chair, gas chamber, or injection. In the Old West they used lynching. Some countries use a firing squad. The Romans crucified. And the Jews stoned. But the Phoenicians had a most unique way of capital punishment. They tied a rope around a man's neck and then tied the other end of the rope to a huge stone and cast both of them over a cliff and into the sea. The weight of the stone would drag the person to the bottom of the sea, and he would drown. That was Jesus' way of impressing upon us the seriousness of our influence.

When William Culbertson died, his lifelong friend, Edwin Bustard, said of him, "He never caused the enemies of the Lord to blaspheme because of misconduct." We must never cause the enemies of God to blaspheme, but we must also never cause the friends of God to stumble. We have a responsibility for both.

The psalmist expressed the gravity of this thought when he prayed in essence, "Lord, don't let me be a stumbling block to those who trust in you. Don't let me confuse those who are seeking after you" (see Ps. 69:6).

Some Christians are woefully careless in matters of example and, by their carelessness, contribute to the downfall of others. We've heard that classic line, "What's a nice girl like you doing in a place like this?" The world must sometimes wonder the same thing about us. The world does not expect us to be perfect, but it does expect us to be different and to be consistent. We need to practice what we preach, live what we believe. The world doesn't understand it when we don't.

A Principle to Guide Us

Finally, Jesus gives us a guiding principle for being a good influence. It is the principle of sacrifice. We should be willing to relinquish any personal right for the sake of others. When Jesus said, "Then is the Son free?" he claimed to be free from the obligation of paying the Temple tax. Yet he yielded that right for the sake of others. The King brought himself to the place of submission lest he cast a shadow of doubt over his messiahship. His concern for others was greater than his concern for himself.

This willingness to relinquish personal rights in the interest of others is the way of Christ. It is to be our way also (1 Cor. 8:9-13; 9:12; 10:28; Rom. 14:20-23).

This principle will help us in making decisions of right and wrong. Christianity is not a matter of rules and regulations but of principles. As God's free men, we have been set free from the law, and we are governed by love—love for God and love for our neighbor.

The Bible is not like the official rule book for an athletic contest. The athletic rule book not only gives the general rules of the game but attempts to cover every conceivable situation that might arise. If the Bible were that kind of rule book, it would be so heavy we would get a hernia from carrying it around. Jesus, through his death on the cross, set us free from legalism, and now we are to live our lives in consistency with love for God and love for our fellowman. Yielding our rights for the sake of others is consistent with love. It is love in action.

There are five principles that will help us in making decisions of right and wrong and thus in protecting our influence.

First, the principle of Scripture—what does the Bible say? There are some things that are always right and some things that are always wrong. They are the eternal absolutes of God. On some things like lying, stealing, and adultery, God speaks clearly. We must seek to square our lives by the word of God. We must know and do what the Bible says.

Second, the principle of secrecy—do I want to conceal my actions from other people? If I am doing something I want to

INFLUENCE: An Offense to None

hide, something I do not want other people to know about, something I am ashamed of, then it is probably wrong. If I cannot do it with a clear conscience, out in the open without guilt or shame, it probably has no place in my life.

Third, the principle of stewardship — will doing this harm my body? My body does not belong to me. It belongs to Jesus Christ. He purchased it by his death on the cross. When I accepted Christ, his Holy Spirit came to dwell in me, and now my body is his temple. I must not do anything to defile it. I must be a good steward of the temple over which I am a custodian. I should ask myself about all questions, "How will this affect my body? Will it contribute to good health and the building of a strong body?" The body is far more important than we realize. It is an asset or a liability all the days of our life. A healthy body can be a wonderful servant. A sickly body can be a terrible monster. I must take care of my body as a good steward of God.

Fourth, the principle of supplication — what does God say to me through prayer? The word *supplication* means "to ask." I should consult God about all matters. I should ask for his guidance in what is right and what is wrong.

Finally, the principle of sacrifice — how will this affect others? I will do what I do not have to do in order to be a good influence. And I will be willing to give up what is enjoyable and even harmless to me if it will hurt someone else who is less mature than I. A banker friend of mine said at his bank they have a saying, "People don't do what's expected. They do what's inspected." But that should not be true of a Christian. This principle indicates that the Christian always does more than is expected. And his life can stand inspection.

We must recognize that not all people are at the same level of maturity. We need to ask ourselves, "Will doing a thing or not doing it hurt those who are less mature than I? Will my participation make it easier or more difficult for me to witness to my unsaved friend about Christ? Would an unsaved person expect me to do this? How will my participation in this affect the cause of Christ?" Then, on the basis of these questions and answers, I make my decision. A religion of rule says "You must." But Christian principles say "I will."

This is not to suggest that you should let every neurotic around determine everything you do. No matter what you do, there are apt to be some people who will find fault in it. However, you must seek always to maintain a life-style that sets the right kind of example.

To become all that God wants us to be in character and in career, we must learn the principle of sacrifice. This principle finds its ultimate expression in Jesus Christ and his death upon the cross. He did not have to die. He could have called more than twelve legions of angels to save him. But he yielded his rights for our benefit. We now must be willing to do the same for him and for others.

Note

1. Paul Gilbert, "Your Own Version," *Masterpieces of Religious Verse* (Nashville: Broadman Press, 1977), p. 362.

8
GRACE
The Bottom Line of Discipleship

The term *bottom line* is technically a business term that means the final assessment, the net result, of a business transaction. It is the dollar amount on a balance sheet after all expenses have been paid. It is the final profit and loss figure of an entire business operation.

Today the term *bottom line* is used by almost everyone. It has been picked up by writers, commentators, critics, and coaches to describe the final evaluation of an effort. We are so geared to think in terms of the "bottom line" in everyday life that it is difficult for us not to think in those terms about spiritual things. When it comes to following Christ we want to know, "What is the bottom line of discipleship?"

That was the question on Peter's mind when he asked Jesus, "Behold, we have forsaken all, and followed thee; what shall we have therefore?" (Matt. 19:27). Peter wanted to know what he and his friends were going to get out of discipleship.

Saved by Grace

A look at the experience preceding this question will help us to understand it better. A young man asked Jesus, "Good Master, what good thing shall I do, that I may have eternal life?" (Matt. 19:16). This young man had a lot going for him. He had youth, wealth, and prominence. But with all that he was not happy. Something was missing from his life. He did not have the peace, satisfaction, and fulfillment that he wanted.

His question reveals two things. First, it reveals his estimate of Jesus. In referring to Jesus as "good," he used the title that belonged only to God. Second, it reveals his estimate of the way to have eternal life. Like the Pharisees, he thought in terms of keeping rules and regulations. He thought of piling up credit on a balance sheet with God by keeping the works of the law. He knew nothing of grace. He thought that by doing some good thing he could earn eternal life. He wanted "merit" with God, and he was ready to make the effort.

The response of Jesus was intended to probe his thinking to see if he really realized what he had said. Did he understand it? Did he really mean it? He asked, "Why callest thou me good? there is none good but one, that is, God" (Matt. 19:17).

To make his point, Jesus then sent the young man back to what had already been revealed in the law. He told him to "keep the commandments."

The young man asked, "Which?" Jesus then stated five of the Ten Commandments. He said, "Thou shalt do no murder, Thou shalt not commit adultery, Thou shalt not steal, Thou shalt not bear false witness, Honour thy father and thy mother: [then he added] and, Thou shalt love thy neighbour as thyself" (Matt. 19:18-19).

All of these are from the second half of the Ten Commandments. The first four of the Ten Commandments deal with our duty to God. The second six deal with our relationships to our fellow man. They are summed up in the command, "Thou shalt love thy neighbour as thyself" (Matt. 19:19). This was obviously the point at which the young man was having the greatest difficulty in his life.

The young man then replied, "All these things have I kept from my youth up: what lack I yet?" This is not a brazen boast.

GRACE: The Bottom Line of Discipleship

He simply thought that observing the externals constituted keeping the Law, and he had done this. But there was still inward dissatisfaction. He had tried legalism without fulfillment. Now he wanted to know what else he could do. Whatever it was, he was ready to do it.

So Jesus said to him, "If you want to be completely happy, go and sell all that you have, and give it to the poor and you will have treasure in heaven: then come and follow me" (see Matt. 19:21).

At first, that seems to be a strange command. There are many righteous men in the Scriptures who had wealth, and they were not commanded to give it all away. Abraham was a rich man. Job was one of the wealthiest men in the East. Joseph of Arimathea and Nicodemus were well off. Zacchaeus was one of the wealthiest men of Jericho. Jesus never commanded them to give everything away. The reason was that they owned their wealth. But this young man's wealth owned him.

The words of Jesus unmasked the young man's real problem by demonstrating one of his faults. Beyond all of the good things he had done, he had a greedy, grasping spirit. So he was commanded to sell everything that he had, and then the man was given a positive invitation to put his faith and trust in Christ and to follow after him.

This young man was unwilling to do that, and so he walked away from Christ sorrowfully. He made a great refusal because he had great riches.

This was a striking example of the seductive power of wealth. So, Jesus seized upon the opportunity to teach his disciples the peril of riches. He then told them it was very hard for a rich man to enter into the kingdom of heaven. To reinforce this teaching, he gave them the proverb, "It is easier for a camel to go through the eye of a needle than for a rich man to enter into the kingdom of God." This was a comical figure of speech to illustrate truth.

Riches can greatly increase the difficulty of entering the kingdom of God—not because they are sinful, but because they are dangerous. Riches encourage a false independence. Because in the world wealth means power and power creates pride, it is hard for the rich to have the right perspective and to be saved. Jesus said, "Blessed are the poor in spirit for theirs is the kingdom of heaven" (Matt. 5:3). It is hard for the rich and powerful to be poor in spirit.

Riches can shackle us to this earth. Samuel Johnson once walked through the beautiful gardens of a stately mansion. As he observed the beauty around him he said, "These are the things which make it hard to die." It is possible to be so interested in earthly things that we forget about heavenly things. And riches can make a person selfish. It is human nature to want more. Enough is always a little bit more than one has. When a person has wealth and luxury, he begins to fear he will lose it. Instead of sharing it he clings to it. He tries to gain more and more to guarantee his security. All of this makes it hard to turn loose and trust Jesus only for salvation.

This teaching amazed the disciples. They held to the popular belief that wealth was a sign of God's favor. They thought that if the wealthy would have a difficult time being saved, the poor would have no chance at all. So they asked Jesus, "Who then can be saved?"

Jesus responded, "With men it is impossible; but with God all things are possible." Salvation does not come by wealth, power, influence, or by piling up credit on a balance sheet with God. There is nothing we can do to merit our salvation. It is the work and the gift of God alone. Salvation is by grace.

Service by Grace

It is at this point that Peter asked about the bottom line of discipleship. He reminded Jesus that he and the other disci-

GRACE: The Bottom Line of Discipleship

ples had forsaken all to follow him. Now he wanted to know, "What's in it for us?" He was saying that they had done exactly what Jesus had told this young man to do. They were not wealthy, but they had forsaken everything that they had. That's all any person can do. Now he wanted to know the net result, the end product, the bottom line of discipleship.

This question was typical of Peter. He was never without words, never tongue-tied, always apt to blurt out whatever was on his mind. He had made great sacrifices for the cause of Christ. Now he wanted to know the benefits.

You might have expected Jesus to rebuke him. He might have said, "The person who follows me with that kind of spirit has no idea what it means to be my disciple." However, Jesus did not do that. He recognized this as a normal reaction and answered it forthrightly.

If Peter were to achieve his highest potential in character and in career, he needed to know the bottom line of discipleship. So, Jesus proceeded to tell him that those who follow him would receive three things.

First, we will receive a new future. In the regeneration, that is, the new world, we will assist him in ruling and administering his kingdom.

Second, we will receive a new family. The church is the family of God. Through being born again, we enter into a new fellowship—human and divine. Many of these early disciples had to give up their friends and their family, but they entered into a wider circle of friendship and fellowship when they began following Christ.

Third, we will receive a new fulfillment. We will inherit everlasting life—the life that the rich young ruler had sought and missed. Peter is assured he'll get more than he gave up.

Jesus is not through yet. He goes on to say, "But many that are first shall be last; and the last shall be first." The word *but* is a transitional word. With it, Jesus moves from the promised rewards to a gentle rebuking of a mercenary spirit.

To illustrate what he means Jesus tells the simple story of the laborers in a vineyard (Matt. 20:1-6). An employer went out early in the morning to hire laborers to work in his vineyard. The marketplace also served as a labor yard, so laborers went there to make themselves available for employment. When he found a group of men, they contracted to work for a penny a day. That was the standard wage for a laboring man. So he sent these men into his vineyard.

About nine o'clock, he returned to the marketplace and some others were standing idle. He hired them and sent them to work in his vineyard with the promise that he would pay them whatever was right. They had no stated wage, no contract. They went to work with nothing but faith and trust in the fairness of their employer.

Then at twelve o'clock, and three o'clock, he did the same thing. Finally, at five o'clock in the evening, just one hour before quitting time, he went back to the marketplace and found more laborers standing idle. He asked them why they weren't working. They responded that it was because no one had hired them. They had probably gone from marketplace to marketplace all day without any success in finding a job. So he hired them and sent them into his vineyard with the promise that whatever was right he would pay them. They, too, went to work without a contract. They worked by faith alone. Six o'clock came, and it was time to quit work. The foreman called the laborers together to pay them their wages. It was customary in those days to pay laborers at the end of the working day. The poor lived from day to day and were never able to save up enough for the future. So they needed each day's pay after each day's labor.

The employer made one mistake. Those who came last were paid first. This is where he got into trouble. If he had just paid the full-time men first, they would have gone home without knowing the good fortune of the latecomers. But he paid the five o'clock men first. Not only that, he paid them a full day's wages. And he paid the three o'clock men and the twelve o'clock men and the nine o'clock men the same wage. By this time those who had worked all day long were excited. They could imagine receiving a vast salary for their work. But to their utter amazement, he paid them the same wage he had paid everyone else. So they began to complain. They said, "We worked all day long and through the heat of the day and you paid those who worked only one hour as much as you paid us" (see Matt. 20:12).

The employer protested, "I didn't do anything wrong. You contracted with me for a certain wage, and I paid you that. A deal is a deal. A bargain is a bargain. I did what we agreed upon. So, take your pay and move on. Don't I have a right to do what I want to do with my own money? I haven't cheated you. I have simply been generous to the other laborers. Do you look upon me as evil for that?"

Then Jesus repeats what he said to Peter earlier. "So the last shall be first, and the first last" (Matt. 20:16). The purpose of this parable was to show Peter and all of us the spirit in which we are to work for God. We are not to work by contract but by faith. We are to trust God completely to do what is right. Peter's mercenary spirit was like those first laborers who worked by contract. We are to be like the later laborers who worked with no assurance but the word of their employer.

This parable is not intended to teach us a lesson in economics. It was not given to tell us how to carry on our business in everyday life. It is intended to teach us the economics of the kingdom of God. It teaches that the bottom line of discipleship is grace. Salvation is by grace and rewards are by grace.

We must guard against that mercenary spirit that is always asking, "What am I going to get out of it?" Those who work for rewards will never get as much as they want. But those who work for love always get more than they expect. Jesus assures us that we will be amply rewarded if we follow him. But the important thing is that we must not let this be our main concern. We must work by faith and believe that God will do what is just. Like those last servants, it is enough for us that he has said, "Whatsoever is right I will give you" (Matt. 20:4).

This parable exposes the wrong spirit of Peter and the disciples and shows us the right spirit for all Christian service.

Greed is always destructive. Several months ago, I was on a plane with a group of businessmen who were playing gin rummy. One of the men was trying to decide whether to lay his cards down or draw again. A third man who was watching the game cautioned him, "Pigs get fat, but hogs get slaughtered." Greed works that way. It ends up devouring us if we are not careful. We must not let the bargaining spirit be the motivating force of our living, serving or giving.

Surprised by Grace

Twice in this teaching Jesus said, "But many that are first shall be last; and the last shall be first." What did he mean by that statement? It suggests that when we get to the bottom line of discipleship there will not only be abundant rewards but also some amazing reversals. Heaven will be full of surprises.

In the parable the employer told the laborers, "Go into the vineyard, and whatever is right I will give you" (see Matt. 20:4). They took him at his word. They trusted his honesty and his fairness, and their confidence was more than rewarded. It was surprisingly rewarded. We can labor with that same kind of confidence.

God deals with us not on the grounds of merit and strict justice alone but on the basis of grace. What is grace? It is unmerited favor. It is receiving what we do not deserve. It is getting the full day's pay for a partial day's labor.

GRACE: The Bottom Line of Discipleship

Years ago, when one of my sons was just a little boy, he stole some pencils from our neighborhood grocery store. He didn't need the pencils. It was just one of those foolish boyish acts. When I discovered the theft, I took him to the grocery store and made him confess to the owner and then pay for the pencils. The grocery store owner, who knew us well, took the money and then reprimanded my son.

It just so happened that it was my son's birthday, and the groceryman knew it. So after he had finished scolding him, he shoved the money back across the counter and said to him, "Happy Birthday, Kent!"

That's grace! It's receiving what you do not deserve. It's a gift when you deserve a gripe. God operates on the basis of grace. He does not give us what we deserve or work for but what we really need.

Recently a news reporter questioned me about the fate of the heathen. He wanted to know what would happen to those who have never heard of Jesus Christ—those sincere people of other religions on the dark continents of the earth who have never heard the gospel. My answer is always the same: "You can trust God to do what is right. On the judgment day, no one will be able to look God in the face and honestly say, 'You were not fair with me.'"

To me, the really amazing thing is not that in eternity some shall be lost but that any shall be saved. John Newton, who wrote "Amazing Grace," said, "I expect to find three wonders in heaven. First, to meet some I had not thought to find there. Second, to miss some I had thought to find there. Third, the greatest wonder of all, to find myself there."

Although the rewards of discipleship are certain and generous, there will be many surprises.

What then is the bottom line of discipleship? It is grace. We are saved by grace. We are to serve by grace. And we shall be surprised by grace.

According to a legend, Thomas Aquinas was addressed by Jesus while in his devotions one day: "Thomas, thou hast written much and well concerning me. What shall I give thee for thy work?"

He answered, "Nothing but thyself, O Lord."

When that is enough for us also, we will be making real progress toward our highest capability in life.

9
FORGIVENESS
Initial and Continual Cleansing

God is no respecter of persons, but he is a respecter of character. God can and will use any of us in his service, but to achieve our highest usefulness our lives must be clean.

The apostle Paul taught this truth through a simple illustration. He said that in a mansion there are many different kinds of dishes. Some are made of gold, some of silver, some of wood, and some of pottery. Some of these dishes are used by the servants and some of them are reserved exclusively for the master of the house and for the entertainment of special guests on special occasions.

Then Paul suggests that we are like dishes. We are all different, but the one thing necessary for our usefulness to God is that we be clean. He wrote to Timothy, "If a man therefore purge [cleanse] himself from these, he shall be a vessel unto honor, sanctified, and meet for the master's use, and prepared unto every good work" (2 Tim. 2:21).

Think about it for a moment. What is the most important thing about a dish that is set before you? It is not its size, nor its shape, nor its color, nor what it is made of. The most important thing about a dish that is set before us is that it be clean. No one wants to eat out of a dirty dish. If the dish is to be fit for our use, it must be clean. It is the same with God. God cannot and will not use dirty vessels in his service. Therefore, to achieve our highest usefulness we must experience both the initial and the continual cleansing from sin.

Jesus taught this in an experience that occurred in the last week of his life (John 13:1-15). The end was near, and he was painfully aware of it. He was meeting with his disciples in the upper room to observe the Passover. You might think that the disciples would be sensitive to what was happening in Jesus' life and that the supper would have begun in a quiet mood. But such was not the case, for in that crucial hour the disciples were squabbling over which one of them would be greatest in the kingdom of God. Jesus had taught them repeatedly that service, not authority, was the mark of greatness in his kingdom, but they obviously had not learned this lesson. They were still quibbling over who would be first among them.

Jesus finally got down on his hands and knees and began to wash his disciples' feet. He performed the menial service of a slave to burn into their minds that he had called them to serve and not to rule. It was while he was in the midst of this experience that he taught Simon and all of us the importance of cleansing in the Christian life.

When he came to Simon's feet, Peter said to him, "Lord, dost thou wash my feet?" (John 13:6). This was a question of astonishment. The emphasis in the Greek is placed on the two pronouns *thou* and *my*. Peter cannot believe that Jesus is going to wash his feet.

Jesus responded, "You do not understand what I am doing now, but you will later on" (see John 13:7). With that statement, Jesus suggests that there is more here than meets the eye. It lifted the act from one of menial service to one of spiritual significance. Peter could easily understand the outward service Christ was about to render to him. But the spiritual significance of it he failed to perceive. Outwardly Jesus was teaching them the importance of humble service. In fact, he tells them exactly what he was doing when he says, "For I have given you an example, that you should do as I have done unto you" (v. 15). But there was a depth of meaning

FORGIVENESS: Initial and Continual Cleansing

here that they could not yet perceive. It would be made plain after the crucifixion and the resurrection.

Still Peter insisted, "You shall never wash my feet." Jesus responded, "If I wash you not, you have no part of me" (see v. 8). To have a part with Jesus was to share in his reign, his glory, and his love. To have no part with him was to be forever separated from God. This was unthinkable to Peter. So, he makes a complete reversal in attitude. In an action that is thoroughly characteristic of the bold and impulsive Peter, he swings to the opposite extreme. He says, "Lord, if that is the case, then wash not only my feet, but also my hands and my head" (see John 13:9).

It is at this point that Jesus gives Peter a little vignette to teach him about spiritual cleansing. He said to him, "He that is washed needeth not [to be washed again] save to wash his feet, but is clean every whit: and ye are clean, but not all" (John 13:10); that is, "you are all clean except Judas, who has betrayed me."

At first reading, this is a difficult parable to comprehend. The difficulty is due to the translation of the word *wash*. The same English word is used twice. However, in the Greek, these are two different words. The word *washed* in the first part of the verse is better translated *bathed*. It indicates a complete cleansing. The word for *wash* in the second phrase is better translated *rinse*. It indicates a partial cleansing.

So, Jesus was saying to Peter, "A person who has bathed does not need to bathe again, but only to have his feet rinsed off, and then he will be clean all over."

The idea behind this is that then, as now, before people went out to dinner at night, they customarily took a bath. But in those days there were no sidewalks or paved streets. And the shoes of ordinary people were simply soles held on the foot by a few leather straps. They gave little protection against the dust and mud of the road. So as a person traveled from his home to his dinner engagement, his feet would get dirty. Since people did not sit in chairs as we do, but rather reclined on pillows and often even drew their feet up under them as they reclined, clean feet were important. For this reason, the host provided great water pots at the door of his house, and often a servant was there with a laver and towel to wash the soiled feet of his guests as they came in. They did not need to take a bath. They had already had that. They needed only to wash their feet which had become dusty on the road.

The foot washing by Jesus signified more than the removal of dust from the disciples' feet. It was symbolical of spiritual cleansing. With one exception, the disciples had been renewed in heart. They had passed from death unto life. They had been saved by the washing of regeneration, and their sins had been forgiven. But they were not yet delivered from all evil. So they need a continual cleansing of the travel stains of life.

Jesus was saying to Peter, "You have already been cleansed of your sins. That happened when you became my disciple. Your sins have been washed away through the bath of salvation. You have been saved once, and there is no need for that to be repeated. But you do need a day-to-day cleansing from the sin and defilement that you pick up as you walk along life's way. Now you need to be washed of the self-seeking attitude that you have been displaying. You need to be rinsed of your proud and arrogant spirit."

The first washing symbolizes the full and complete cleansing of regeneration that occurs when we come to Christ for salvation. The second washing [rinsing] symbolizes the daily cleansing from the sins of our daily walk. Without the first washing, we have no relationship with him. WIthout the second washing, we have no fellowship with him. Without the bathing, we are unsaved. Without the rinsing, we are unusable. The first washing takes care of the guilt and sin of the past. The second washing takes care of the defilement of our daily walk. By the first cleansing, we become Christians. By the second cleansing, we become effective witnesses to the world.

We need both the bathing and rinsing in our Christian life. The washing of regeneration makes us clean in God's sight. But further cleansing of the spots of defilement are necessary. Once joined to Christ by his blood, we are completely forgiven, cleansed, and justified. But we all need, every day, as we walk through life, to be cleansed of our daily failures. We need, in short, a daily washing of our sins over and above the great washing of justification which is ours the moment we believe. We need a daily purification from our evil acts and desires. The continual and daily cleansing is a necessary complement to our initial justification. We need the bathing to be saved; we need the rinsing to be of service.

If Peter was ever to become all he was capable of being in character and career in God's kingdom, he must learn the secret of both the initial and the continual cleansing. It is the same with us.

The Cleansing of Conversion

The Bible mentions three kinds of cleansing that we all need. The first is the cleansing of conversion. Paul spoke of this when he said, "Not by works of righteousness which we have done, but according to his mercy he saved us, by the washing of regeneration" (Titus 3:5).

When we become Christians, the Lord does three things for us. First, he gives us hope for the future. Almost every week, I stand by the bedside of someone who has a disease diagnosed as terminal. For Christians, the word *transitional* would better describe their condition. Death to the Christian is not the end. It is our entrance into God's presence. Through conversion, Jesus Christ gives to us eternal life.

Second, he gives us help for the present. This is what most people long for the most. They would quickly say to you, "I know I am going to heaven when I die. But my problem isn't what will happen to me in the future. I believe that God will take care of that. My big problem is the here and now. It is the situation in which I find myself today." Jesus helps us in the present also. At conversion, he comes to be with us and in us. He walks beside us to give us comfort, and he dwells within us to give us strength.

Third, he gives us healing for the past. Peter spoke of the cleansing from past sins when he said, "By whose stripes [wounds] ye were healed" (1 Pet. 2:24).

Sin is like a cancer in our soul that we cannot deal with by ourselves. You cannot unscramble an egg. You cannot unbreak a glass. You cannot unsay a word. And you cannot undo sin. Our only hope is the cleansing and forgiveness of God. By his death and resurrection, Jesus dealt effectively with our sin. He did for us what we were helpless to do for ourselves (Rom. 5:6-8). Through him, there is healing and cleansing.

The Word of God abounds with promises of this. Isaiah writes, "Come now, and let us reason together, saith the Lord: though your sins be as scarlet, they shall be as white as snow; though they be red like crimson, they shall be as wool" (Isa. 1:18). John calls Jesus "the Lamb of God, who takes away the sins of the world" (see John 1:29). After being given a list of the vilest sins, the apostle Paul said, concerning the Corinthian Christians, "And such were some of you: but ye are washed, but ye are sanctified, but ye are justified in the name of the Lord Jesus, and by the Spirit of our God" (1 Cor. 6:11). And John described Jesus as the one who "loved us, washed us from our sins in his own blood" (Rev. 1:5).

How wonderful and complete is the forgiveness of God. He promises to remove our sins as far as the east is from the west

FORGIVENESS: Initial and Continual Cleansing

(Ps. 103:12). He promises to cast our sins into the depths of the sea (Mic. 7:19). And he promises to remember them no more (Jer. 31:34).

That's what God gives us at conversion: hope for the future, help for the present, and healing for the past. That is God's complete redemption. And a part of it is the cleansing, the washing away, of our sins.

The Cleansing of Scripture

In addition to the initial cleansing of conversion, there is also a continual cleansing that can come through the Scriptures.

The psalmist asked the question, "Wherewithal shall a young man cleanse his way?" Then he answers his own question, "By taking heed thereto according to thy word" (Ps. 119:9). Through a continual obedience to God's word, we can experience a continual cleansing in our daily lives.

Two verses later he says, "Thy word have I hid in mine heart, that I might not sin against thee" (v. 11). Where are we to have the word of God? In our home? Yes! In our hand? Yes! In our head? Yes! But, most of all, we are to have it in our hearts. We are to live it out day-by-day. And as we do, it has a cleansing effect upon our lives.

The Word of God is many things to us. It is a mirror to reveal us (Jas. 1:23); milk to nourish us (1 Pet. 2:2); meat to strengthen us (Heb. 5:12); honey to delight us (Ps. 119:103); fire to warm us (Jer. 23:29); a hammer to break us (Jer. 23:29); a knife to expose us (Heb. 4:12); a lamp to guide us (Ps. 119:105); and it is water to wash us (Eph. 5:25-26).

Jesus said, "Now ye are clean through the word which I have spoken unto you" (John 15:3). And Paul speaks of one being washed by the water of the Word (Eph. 5:26). This is a reference to the inward ethical purification that is accompanied by the Word of God having liberty in the heart of believers. As water washes the body, so the Word of God washes the heart.

A Christian complained that when she read the Bible she got nothing out of it whatsoever, and she was tempted to stop reading it. But her preacher said, "Get me a bottle," and she did. "Fill it with water," said the preacher, and she filled it with water. "Now," said the good man, "pour it all out again." And she did. Then the preacher said pointedly, "You have retained nothing in the bottle of that which you poured in,"— and he paused, "but the bottle is much cleaner after the water has passed through it, even though nothing remains of it. So it is with the Word of God. You cannot read it without receiving some blessing, even though you may not be conscious of it at the time."

Gipsy Smith told of a man who said he had received no inspiration from the Bible although he had "gone through it several times." "Let it go through you once," was his reply, "then you will tell a different story!" The evangelist spoke wisely, and his admonition is excellent advice for all who seek full blessings from the Scriptures. Ask the Holy Spirit to apply its precepts to your life, and you will experience its cleansing effect. Through a daily, continual studying of God's word, your life can be rinsed clean of the defilements from your daily walk.

The Cleansing of Confession

Finally, there is a cleansing that comes by confession. John spoke of this cleansing when he said, "If we confess our sins, he is faithful and just to forgive us our sins, and to cleanse us from all unrighteousness" (1 John 1:9). There is really a double promise in this verse. It is the promise of both forgiveness and cleansing. There is a difference in the two. Forgiveness restores our relationship. Cleansing removes our sin. Through forgiveness, we have a relationship with God.

FORGIVENESS: Initial and Continual Cleansing

Through cleansing, we have fellowship with him. There are three marvelous truths concerning forgiveness and cleansing in this passage.

First, the condition of cleansing, "If we confess our sins." The only way to deal with sin is to honestly and openly acknowledge it to God. If we refuse to admit our sin, then we live in a world of illusions. Many people do just that. They make alibis for themselves. They excuse their actions. They rationalize their behavior. They justify their failures. The result is that they never know the forgiveness of God. The Scriptures say, "He that covereth his sins shall not prosper: but whoso confesseth and forsaketh them shall have mercy" (Prov. 28:13). We must first own, then disown, our sins. We must acknowledge them and then abandon them. The same moment which brings a consciousness of sin should also bring the confession of that sin. Like David, we ought to cry out to God. "Blot out my transgressions . . . wash me, and I shall be whiter than snow" (Ps. 51:1,7).

Second, the certainty of cleansing. "He is faithful and just." If we confess our sins, how can we be sure that we are cleansed? What assurance do we have? The grounds of our assurance is the character of God. He is faithful, that is, utterly reliable, and just, that is, straightforward, in his dealings with us. God never lies. He does what he says he will do. Our assurance is not based on our feelings, for they are forever changing. But God is always the same. We can be sure that we are cleansed because God says so.

Third, the completeness of cleansing. He will cleanse us of *all* unrighteousness. Call sin what you like—evil, transgression, wickedness, vice, crime, uncleanness, failure, filth, guilt, bondage, iniquity, stain, wrong, or misdemeanor. Here are fourteen of its many names and aspects. But they are all covered by this one little word *all*. There is no sin beyond his cleansing if we will confess it.

Jesus Christ not only died on the cross for our sins and was raised from the dead for our justification, but he also continues to be active for us now. As our advocate, he intercedes in the court of God in our behalf. He is both our propitiation (covering) and our advocate (attorney). He is the means by which our sins are forgiven and cleansed (1 John 2:1-2).

Here, then, is the way to be both bathed and rinsed. This is God's plan for initial and continual cleansing. Peter needed both of them to become all he was capable of being. We need both of them also.

There are more than seven hundred promises in the Bible. These promises are like sacks of cement. As cement must be mixed with water to be effective, so these promises must be mixed with faith in your life in order to be effective. Claim them and act upon them today, and you can know the initial, continual, and conditional cleansing of God that is necessary to reaching your greatest spiritual potential.

10
WATCHFULNESS
The Sifting of Satan

The Christian life is not a Sunday afternoon stroll but a seven-day-a-week struggle. It is not a pleasant walk but a perilous warfare. People can never achieve their highest potential either in character or in career unless they recognize this. Satan is the opponent, the adversary, the enemy of God and his people. And the more we mean to God, the more we will mean to him. Repeatedly in the Scriptures we are warned of Satan's cunning, his deceitfulness, and his power.

We have an example of this struggle when Jesus said to Peter, "Simon, Simon, behold, Satan hath desired to have you, that he may sift you as wheat: But I have prayed for thee that thy faith will fail not: and when thou art converted, strengthen thy brethren" (Luke 22:31-32).

Jesus and his disciples had gone to Jerusalem where he knew in advance that he would be betrayed and crucified. As they met in the upper room to observe the Passover and inaugurate the Lord's Supper, he told them that one of their group would betray him. Then the Scriptures say that Satan entered into Judas, and he proceeded with his treachery.

It was following this event that Jesus issued his warning to Simon Peter. He wanted him to know of the traumatic experiences he would face in the hours to come. His opponent Satan was going to do everything he could to shake him from his faithfulness to Jesus. And Jesus wanted to assure Peter that in the midst of his conflict he would be praying for him that he would stand the test.

This warning of Jesus is so significant that it is worthy of careful analysis. Jesus begins by calling Peter by his old name "Simon" that symbolized his weakness. The repetition of that name suggested the solemnity of what Jesus was about to say. Satan was going to give him a good shaking.

Have You Met the Devil?

The word *Satan* is an Aramaic word that means "the accuser" or "adversary." If you will take time to read through the Gospel of Luke, you will meet Satan on several occasions before this. He came to Jesus as he fasted and prayed in the wilderness in preparation for his public ministry and tempted him to go away from the will of God. Jesus responded to the temptation by saying, "Get thee behind me, Satan" (Luke 4:8).

Later Jesus describes a woman who has been crippled for eighteen years as one "whom Satan hath bound" (Luke 13:16). And then in this same chapter as the betrayal of Judas is exposed, the narrative states, "Then Satan entered into Judas" (Luke 22:3). Now Jesus warns Peter that Satan wants to sift him as wheat.

So, Satan is described as the tempter, the crippler, the destroyer, and now the sifter.

Many people today do not believe in a personal Satan. They believe that such thinking is a part of mankind's nursery furniture. They put him in the same category as Santa Claus or the Easter Bunny. They relegate him to the superstition of the Middle Ages. It is amazing that a world so tortured and beset by Satan should question his reality or his activity— especially in the light of the repeated affirmations of the Bible concerning his reality. Granted, the truth about Satan has been greatly distorted by the false notions of the past, but that does not nullify his reality.

Where Did Satan Come From?

Satan's origin is only hinted at in the Scriptures. Seemingly, he was an angel created in perfection; but, being filled with pride, he rebelled against God and was cast out of heaven. Thus he became the prince of this world. It is clear that from the very moment of creation, Satan was on the scene as a rebel against God. He appeared to Adam and Eve disguised as a serpent. The most important thing though is not the origin of evil but the fact of evil. Jesus acknowledges that fact here.

While Satan has great power, he does not have unlimited power. Jesus states that Satan "desired" to tempt Peter. The word *desire* can mean to ask excessively. It means to request. Jesus is telling Peter that Satan wants permission to get at him. That's interesting. It underlines the teaching that evil is not ultimate in the universe. The power of Satan is limited both in time and scope. The real force of the Greek verb is "Satan hath obtained you by asking." But he had to ask. Whatever sifting is coming, it is only by divine permission. Satan has great power, but he is not equal to God.

Why Doesn't God Kill the Devil?

If Satan is the enemy of God and his people, why is he allowed to continue? Why doesn't God kill the devil? There are several reasons. First, he allows Satan to exist in order to give us a choice in life. There can be no freedom and no choices without options. If Satan did not exist, then evil would not exist. So it would not be an option. We would be serving God not because we loved him but because we had no other choice.

Again, he allows Satan to exist in order to build our character. It is only as we struggle with temptation, as we grapple with right and wrong, that we ever develop character. Parents who protect their children from every decision and every hardship ultimately send weaklings and fools out into the world. Character is developed only out of conflict and struggle. And it is our character, not our comfort, that God is most interested in.

Finally, he allows Satan to continue to exist to show the ultimate consequences of sin. He is going to allow Satan and sin to run their course so that in eternity the people of God will be able to see and know the fruits of rebellion and sin. If we did not see it, we would never know it for sure. For those reasons he allows Satan to continue to exist. But he operates only in the permissive will of God. He is around for your good and my good. He is around to purify the body of Christ. He is there to sift us and to shake us to see what we are made of.

What Is Satan Doing?

What does Satan want to do to us? What is his goal, his objective? He wants to "sift" us as wheat. Our generation knows very little about sifting. I spent the early years of my life in the country and in small towns. Grocery shopping was done once a week, and bakeries did not exist. So we couldn't run to the corner grocery store every day to buy a loaf of bread, and, believe it or not, in those days canned biscuits hadn't even been invented.

So if we had bread to eat, Mother had to bake it. I think she must have been the best biscuit baker in the whole world. I don't remember ever eating a meal at my home as I was growing up without Mother's homemade biscuits. She had a wooden mixing bowl, and without measuring anything, she would pour in some flour, a pinch of salt, a little shortening and baking soda, add a little buttermilk, and mix up a wonderful batch of biscuits.

In those days, we bought our flour in twenty-five-pound

WATCHFULNESS: The Sifting of Satan

sacks. Oftentimes it was lumpy. So in order to smooth the texture of the flour, Mother would put some of it in a tin sifter and shake it back and forth to get the lumps out. The purpose of sifting was to separate. The method of sifting was shaking.

The word also describes the winnowing process of separating wheat from the chaff in the New Testament time. The violent shaking of wheat to separate it became a symbol of the violent trial Peter would experience as Satan tried to shake him from his faith in Jesus.

This is always the design of Satan. The Bible declares his existence, his intentions, as well as his methods. It tells us that he is a spiritual being who is the enemy of God and his people, and all that is good. And it is his desire to shake us from our faith and to lead us to apostasy.

The adversary asked permission to give Peter a good shaking, and Jesus granted it. But then Jesus assures Peter, "I have prayed for you that your faith fail not." This is amazing! Here is a man that both Satan and Christ want. Satan wants to shake him from his faith; the Lord wants to strengthen him so he won't turn from his faith.

If we ever hope to attain our full possibilities as followers of Christ, like Peter we must realize there are two powers in this world that want us. We must know that we have an adversary as well as an Advocate (1 John 2:1).

Satan has asked for permission, and Jesus will allow it. He will not prevent the shaking, but he will pray for us to be strengthened in the midst of it. How does Satan shake us today? We must not be ignorant of his devices if we are going to grow to our full potential.

Sifted by Doubts

One of the ways Satan attempts to shake us from our faithfulness to Christ is through planting doubts in our minds. From the very first, this has been one of his principle methods of attack. He knows if he can get us to doubt the Word of God, then we can more easily be led to disobey the will of God.

This was the line of attack he took with Adam and Eve. God made it very clear to the first couple that if they disobeyed him, they would die. But Satan called God's word into question when he said, "Ye shall not surely die" (Gen. 3:4). Then he told them that instead of bringing death, the fruit would bring enlightment, divinity, perception, and wisdom. Far from being a dreadful experience, it would be a delightful one. He made sin look so beautiful and desirable that Adam and Eve yielded to his temptation.

He followed the same line of temptation with Jesus. At the outset of his ministry, Jesus went into the wilderness to pray and fast in preparation for his forthcoming work. Satan came to him to attempt to divert him from the will of God. He encouraged Jesus to begin his ministry with the spectacular feat of jumping from the highest point of the Temple to the ground. He assured him that he could not be hurt by quoting the words of the psalmist, "For he shall give his angels charge over thee, to keep thee in all thy ways. They shall bear thee up in their hands, lest thou dash thy foot against a stone" (Ps. 91:11-12).

The quotation was right; the application was wrong. He was distorting the promise of God and attempting to get Jesus to presume on God. Distortions and doubts are still some of his principle tools in leading us to sin. The Word of God has been given to guide us and direct us in the ways of righteousness. Until Satan can either distort it or make us doubt it, he has little chance of leading us into sin.

Sifted by Desires

Another tool of Satan in trying to shake us from God is to appeal to the desires that are deep within us.

WATCHFULNESS: The Sifting of Satan

Carl Sandburg once said, "There's a zoo in me." He was right. There is a whole jungle of wild, ferocious desires in every one of us. And these desires never leave us.

David was a man after God's own heart, and yet he desired Bathsheba and that desire led to sin. Elijah was a great prophet, but he was a man of like passions even as we are (Jas. 5:17). The word *passions* means appetites, weaknesses, frailties. He was a great prophet of God, but he was cut from the same bolt of human cloth as you and I. Even Jesus, the Son of God, was tempted at all points just as we are. That means that he must have had desires and appetites to which Satan could appeal. The differences between Jesus and us is that he never yielded to the temptations. He never gave way to the desires within him (Heb. 4:15).

The appetite I have for one sin or another is the thing that makes temptation possible at all. On the basis of our desires, Satan attempts to draw us away from our dependence on God.

Here is how temptation actually works, "Every man is tempted, when he is drawn away of his own lust, and enticed" (Jas. 1:14). The language here suggests a fish that is swimming a straight course and then is drawn off, lured toward something that seems attractive, only to discover too late that the bait had a deadly hook in it. Satan appeals to our desires and has us hooked quickly.

Where does temptation come from? It doesn't come from God. Don't blame him for it. It comes from our depraved nature. It is from the pull of our own evil thoughts, wishes, and desires. Sin would be helpless if there were nothing in us to which it could appeal. Temptation comes from below and appeals to that which is within to draw us from him who is above.

The writer of Proverbs warns us to guard our heart, for out of it are the issues of life. The Book of Proverbs was written to young men to give them wisdom for daily living. One of the things it often warns them about is sexual sins. It paints a picture of immoral women who lie in wait for the young men. Using flattering words and alluring attire, sweet smelling perfume, and promises of love, they catch the young men who are not thinking.

The end result is, "He goeth after her straightway, as an ox goeth to the slaughter, or as a fool to the correction of the stocks; Till a dart strike through his liver; as a bird hasteth to the snare, and knoweth not that it is for his life" (Prov. 7:5-27). Through appealing to his desires, she hooks him. Perhaps that's the way we got the word *hooker*.

The temptation to sin rarely appears as terrible or undesirable or evil. If so, none of us would ever respond to it. We are not tempted by the disgusting things of sin but the desirable things. Jerry Reuben has been credited with a philosophy, "If it feels good, do it." But he is not the originator of it. That has been Satan's philosophy from the beginning. Reuben did not originate it; he only verbalized it.

Shaken Through Disappointments

Another tool Satan uses in his efforts to shake us from our faith is disappointments. John the Baptist came preaching the nearness of the messianic reign. When he saw Jesus, he said, "Behold the Lamb of God, who takes away the sins of the world" (see John 1:29). He boldly declared Jesus to be the Son of God. Then came his imprisonment. Because of his outspoken preaching against the sins of the king, he was cast into prison. In prison he had a great deal of time to think, to reflect on the life and the ministry of Jesus. When Jesus did not measure up to John's expectations, John actually doubted his identity. Isn't that the case with most of us? When the Lord or someone else does not do what we expect, we face our times of severest doubt and shaking.

John, who announced the Messiah, is now doubting that Jesus is the Messiah. John preached judgment. There is an awful lot of judgment per square inch in his preaching. Some people think that God is not in a place unless there is the smell of fire and brimstone. But Jesus told his disciples to tell John that the blind see, the deaf hear, and the poor have the gospel preached unto them. He was saying, "John, these are the Messiah's work also." Jesus was the Messiah John predicted, but he was not the Messiah John expected.

When the Lord or his people do not measure up to our expectations, it disappoints us. These disappointments can shake us from our faith. A few weeks ago, one of my deacons and his wife called saying they needed to see me immediately. From the look on their faces when they walked into my office, I would have thought someone had just died. I guess in a sense that is what had happened. They sat down and told me of their dear friend and former pastor who had just left his wife for another woman. They had had such great admiration for and confidence in him that they were going through a grief experience that was very much akin to death itself.

If you fix your eyes upon men, sooner or later you will be disappointed. But if you fix your eyes upon Jesus, he will never disappoint you. Paul writes concerning Jesus, "Whosoever believeth on him shall not be ashamed" (Rom. 10:11). The word *ashamed* actually means "to be put to shame" or "to be disappointed." The person who puts his faith and trust in Jesus Christ will never have any cause to be disappointed, either in time or in eternity. He never fails us, either in life or in death. Men may, but Jesus won't.

Shaken by Deceit

Deceit is another method Satan uses to try to shake us from our faithfulness. He is the father of all lies. He has never been limited to the truth. He is a clever trickster who will stop at no deception or lie to trap us and shake us from God's purposes.

Satan promises what he cannot produce. In the mind of the prodigal son, he painted a picture of excitement and glamor beyond anything that could be found around the father's place. But when the boy sat down at the devil's table, he got food poisoning. When the glitter and glamor rubbed off sin, he found himself in a desperate situation. There is no doubt that there is pleasure in sin; the Bible affirms this (Heb. 11:25). But what Satan doesn't tell you is that sin's pleasure is short-lived and costly. He shows you his best first and saves his worst for last. Christ is the opposite. He always saves the best till last.

The devil's lies are not all-out lies. They are half-truths. That perhaps is the most dangerous kind of lie. You are more apt to miss an appointment when your clock is five minutes off than when it is five hours off. The closer a thing is to the truth, the more apt you are to be deceived by it. Sin never comes to us as a terrible and undesirable evil.

Don't Argue, Quote!

When Satan's siftings come, how are we to stand against them? Where can we turn for help? What is our best defense when Satan assaults us? We should follow the example of Jesus. Every time Satan came to Jesus with a temptation, he met the temptation with a quotation from the Word of God. He flatly refused to get involved beyond that. There is no more dangerous moment than the moment of uncertainty and hesitation. Once we consider the temptation of Satan a live option, as a desirable possibility, we are in trouble. So when Satan tempts you, don't argue, quote!

James gave us good advice when he said, "Submit yourselves therefore to God. Resist the devil, and he will flee from you" (Jas. 4:7). Peter was a seasoned and mature Christian

WATCHFULNESS: The Sifting of Satan

warrior who wrote the same instructions, "Be alert, be on watch! Your enemy, the Devil, roams around like a roaring lion, looking for someone to devour" (1 Pet. 5:8, TEV). Here is a twofold plan for dealing with the problem of temptation. The first part is to watch. Remain actively alert for the enemy, vigilant for any move on his part. The second part is to pray. Keep the lines of communication open to headquarters, ever ready to appeal for help.

Whether he comes to you through doubt, disappointments, desires, or deceit, Satan's purpose is always the same. It is to separate you from your faith in and fellowship with Jesus Christ. You must recognize him and resist him, and he will retreat from you.

The more serious we are about growing in the character of Christ, the more temptations we are certain to face. "But," you say, "wouldn't it be better if God gave you some kind of immunity from temptation when we become Christians? Then we'd never fall."

No, not at all! If all things work together for good to them that love God—so does temptation. The good that can result from it is our own spiritual growth. Temptation is a necessary part of our spiritual development. Peter could never become all that Jesus predicted without struggling with temptation. Neither can we. Commitment to Christ means conflict with Satan. That much is unavoidable. But conflict builds character. If we are to climb to our greatest spiritual heights, we must do it in the face of opposition. Through Satan's sifting we struggle, and through struggling we grow strong. That's inherent in the Saint Peter Principle.

11
HUMILITY
Overcome by Overconfidence

Your self-concept is at the core of your personality. It affects everything you do—your conduct, your ability to learn, your growth, your choice of friends, your choice of a mate, and even your career. It is no exaggeration to say that a strong positive self-image is the best possible preparation for a successful life.

While it is good to have self-confidence, it is dangerous to be overconfident. If self-confidence is the first step to success, overconfidence is the first step to failure. The kind of pride and arrogance that keeps people from recognizing and acknowledging their weaknesses has been the downfall of many an otherwise great person.

William Manchester, in his book *American Caesar,* says concerning General Douglas MacArthur,

> He had the strength and power, he meant to bear rule over others and he expected tribute from them. His manifest self-regard, his complete lack of humility, lay like a deep fissure at his very core. In the end it split wide open and destroyed him.[1]

In his book *A Time To Heal,* former President Gerald Ford points out that Richard Nixon "had a brilliant mind, a great sensitivity to the public's political mood and a unique ability to analyze foreign-policy issues and to act decisively on them."[2]

HUMILITY: Overcome by Overconfidence   113

He had many qualities necessary to make a great president.

But he also had a great weakness. President Ford said of him, "Most of us have hidden flaws or personality quirks that seldom come to the surface. . . . In Nixon's case, that flaw was pride. A terribly proud man, he detested weakness in other people."[3] In the end it was that pride, that unwillingness to recognize and acknowledge his own mistakes in the Watergate case, that led to his downfall.

He had not known about the break-in at Watergate beforehand. He found out shortly after it happened. "And I could see why he felt trapped. Some of the people involved . . . were friends of his, and he didn't want to force them to pay the consequences. His pride was stronger than his recognition that he had made a mistake. He viewed admitting the truth in this matter as a sign of weakness, and that was another mistake."[4]

It is always dangerous to be so proud that we do not see and admit our own weaknesses. It is so very easy to stumble over pride—to be overcome by overconfidence.

This is one of the lessons Peter had to learn in his spiritual development. If he were ever going to achieve his highest potential in character and in career, he would have to be aware of and deal with his own weakness.

Jesus taught him this in one of the most tragic episodes in the New Testament. Jesus had met with his disciples to observe the Passover and then the Lord's Supper. Judas had been exposed as the one who would betray his master, and he left the meeting to complete the transaction.

Then Jesus and the other disciples left the upper room and started toward the Mount of Olives. As they walked along the way, Jesus delivered his final warning to them. He told them that they would all be offended because of him that very night. The word *offend* here means "to make to fall away, to cause one to stumble." Jesus knew that the events that were about to happen would cause such fear, disbelief, and despair among his disciples that every one of them would desert him in his hour of greatest need.

To substantiate his warning he quoted the prophet Zechariah, "I will smite the shepherd, and the sheep of the flock shall be scattered abroad" (Matt. 26:31, see Zech. 13:7).

But Peter, always the outspoken one, the bold, impulsive, fiery one, could not yet believe this about himself. Yes, he could believe the others would desert Jesus, but he wouldn't. He expressed his overwhelming self-confidence by saying, "Though all these other men shall desert you, I never will" (see Matt. 26:33).

Jesus responded by saying to him, "Peter, this very night, before the cock crows, you will deny me three times" (see Matt. 26:34). But even this personal warning of Jesus did not convince Peter of his weakness. He was ardent in his claim. "I will die for you, but I will not deny you" (see Matt. 26:35).

Peter was saying in effect, "If I do not know myself, who does know me?" And he was absolutely sincere in this claim. But the one thing a man does not fully know is himself. The Scriptures say, "The heart is deceitful above all things, and desperately wicked; who can know it?" (Jer. 17:9). Peter did not know his own weakness. He knew he loved Jesus. There was never any doubt about that. But he did not know the forces that would be coming against him that night. He did not know how dark the darkness would be. His besetting sin was his self-confidence. He was too sure of himself and ultimately was overcome because of his overconfidence.

This is a danger we all face. The Scriptures warn, "Wherefore let him that thinketh he standeth take heed lest he fall" (1 Cor. 10:12). This is a warning against overconfidence in ourselves and underestimating our enemy. The possibility of

HUMILITY: Overcome by Overconfidence 115

evil lies sleeping in all our hearts. It is coiled like a snake ready to strike at any moment. The potential for sin in all of us is like the dry kindling of a forest waiting for sparks to set it off.

Let no man say in foolish self-confidence that any form of sin which others have committed is impossible for him. There is in your heart and mine the potential for any sin that anyone else has ever committed. And we are in our greatest danger when we think otherwise.

Let the circumstances be right, and there is nothing beyond any one of us. All sin grows out of a few desires and emotions that are within all of us. Cain, in a fit of jealous anger, killed his brother Abel. Is there any jealousy in you? Do you have even a slight temper? If so, those emotions can explode into the same kind of violence in you that it did in Cain. You are capable of murder.

David, the man after God's own heart, marred his own name when he saw the beautiful Bathsheba and lusted after her. He allowed that desire to grow in his mind. Then when the convenient opportunity came he had already made his plans. He invited her to his apartment and committed adultery. To cover up that sin he had her husband sent to the front lines of battle where he would be killed defending his country and his king. This cancer in the palace began with David's lust. The romantic impulse never dies in any of us. Let the circumstances be just right, and we too are capable of that kind of unfaithfulness.

Judas sold Jesus for money. If you have the slightest love of and desire for money, then the possibility of selling Jesus out is within you.

Peter's besetting sin was self-confidence. He boasted that he could not be made to stumble, no, not he! He thought he would rather die than deny his Master. And the other disciples chimed in with the same boast. When one is strong only in himself, then he is at his weakest. The prediction of Jesus was sadly and tragically fulfilled that night. Peter did the very things he said he would never do. And so did the rest of the disciples. Their courage and valor existed only in their imagination. They did not know how much fear was in them. And so when the hour of testing came, they fled.

What happened to them can very well happen to you and me. It is important that we see this. If we do not recognize the potential for evil within us, we will never put our confidence in Christ and thus achieve our highest potential for good.

Overconfidence caused Peter to do the things that very night that led to his failure. It can cause us to stumble the same way.

Watch And Pray!

Jesus and his disciples then went to the garden of Gethsemane. When they arrived, Jesus left most of his disciples at the entrance, and he went inside to pray. He took only Peter, James, and John and asked them to wait and watch with him. Then he went deeper into the garden alone to talk to his Father.

After awhile, he came back to the disciples and found them asleep. He said to Peter, "What, could ye not watch with me one hour? Watch and pray, that ye enter not into temptation: the spirit indeed is willing, but the flesh is weak" (Matt. 26:40-41).

Then Jesus went back into the garden to pray again. He came back the second time and found them asleep once more. Back into the garden he went for another time of agony and prayer. Back he came a third time and found them still asleep.

It was Peter's self-confidence that made him fall asleep even

HUMILITY: Overcome by Overconfidence 117

though Jesus told him to watch and pray lest he enter into temptation. Jesus' statement about the willing spirit and the weak flesh is a recognition of Peter's sincere devotion but his human weakness. The flesh is representative of his weak, sinful nature. And if Peter was to avoid denial, he would have to recognize that weakness and through prayer find the strength necessary to meet temptation.

We must do the same. It is overconfidence that causes us to neglect our prayer life. In the Lord's Prayer, Jesus taught us to pray, "Lead us not into temptation, but deliver us from evil" (Matt. 6:13). Jesus knew that every day, no matter how sheltered we are, we face some choice in which the wrong action is so seductive, so plausible, so pleasurable that it will take God's help to reject it. It is a recognition that at any moment we could trip up and lose everything—self-respect, family, health, position, and even our sanity. To avoid temptation and overcome the evil one, we need God's help. That's why we must pray.

We are no match for Satan on our own. When we think we are, we are most vulnerable to his enticements. It is only as we recognize this that we can hope to win the victory.

Prayer is the gateway to getting help from God. Vance Havner once suggested that prayer is the only thing we can do that affects three worlds at once. It reaches up in worship of God. It reaches out in work to man. And it reaches down in warfare against Satan. It is our overconfidence that causes us to neglect our devotional life, our time of prayer. And, in the final analysis, it is our overconfidence that overcomes us. Self-sufficiency is self-deception. Only God is omnipotent. Everyone has situations of need when he is inadequate. Prayer is a confession of inadequacy. It is a recognition of our limitations. It is the gateway to getting help from God, and if we think we do not need his help we are in the gravest of dangers.

Acting On Your Own

Peter, James, and John were suddenly awakened by the mob that had come to arrest Jesus. When one of the soldiers reached out to take Jesus by the arm, the impulsive Simon Peter took a sword and cut off the man's ear. It never entered his mind to consider the consequences. Doubtlessly, he meant to kill the man, but either the man ducked, or Peter was a poor swordsman.

Peter with a sword in his hand was much like the cross-eyed discus thrower. He didn't set many records, but he sure kept the crowd alert. What Peter was doing was taking matters into his own hands. This kind of temper and impulsiveness is always a sign of pride. Jesus told him to put the sword up. He said, "They that take up the sword shall perish with the sword" (Matt. 26:52). Then he reminded Peter that he could call twelve legions of angels if he wanted to. A full Roman legion consisted of six thousand men. This meant that there were seventy-two thousand angels on alert to assist Jesus at that very moment. Peter had never considered that. He simply took matters into his own hands and did the first thing that came to mind.

Overconfidence always causes us to act on our own. When we do that we are assuming the prerogative of God. Joseph is one of the most admirable characters in all the Bible. If ever a man had reason to try to take matters into his own hands, it was Joseph. Early in his life, he was sold into slavery by his brothers. Later, he was falsely accused of assault by his employer's wife. Then, in an hour of great need, he was forgotten by a man he had befriended. Being rejected by one's own brothers, falsely accused by a woman, and forgotten by a friend would be reason enough for bitterness in anyone.

However, when the opportunity came to strike back, Jo-

HUMILITY: Overcome by Overconfidence

seph refused to do so saying, "Am I in the place of God?" (Gen. 50:19). Joseph realized that if he tried to get even he would be playing God. He would be taking matters into his own hands, and this was the height of presumption. The kind of overconfidence that makes us think we know better than God will lead to our downfall.

Walking, Standing, Sitting!

When the disciples realized that Jesus was actually going to be arrested, they fled in panic. The fear, despair, and disappointment was too much for them, and they ran off into the darkness of the night. As the disciples looked on from the distance, they saw the crowd begin to move slowly toward the place of trial. Peter decided to follow. He should have stayed in hiding, but he was curious to know what was going to happen.

There are times when the best approach to a situation is to run. The Bible says that we are to "flee . . . youthful lusts" (2 Tim. 2:22). It teaches us to stay away "from all appearance of evil" (1 Thess. 5:22).

But Peter's self-confidence made him think, *I know when to stop. I will go only so far, and it will do no harm.* So he began by following the crowd from a great distance. When they arrived at the high priest's palace, Peter stood watching the proceedings. Then, slowly, he moved inside and sat down by the fire so he could hear better (Matt. 26:58).

First, he was walking with the enemy; next he was standing with them; then he was sitting with them. He had flung himself into the very face of temptation. Ordinarily, it would have been proper to follow the Master, but in the light of the fact that he had been warned of a coming defection he ought to have avoided the occasion altogether. So, while Jesus was being tried by Caiaphas, Peter also was being tried by Satan (Luke 22:31).

Walking, standing, and sitting with the wrong crowd is the sad commentary of many a fallen person. David, who knew bitter defeat at the hands of Satan, wrote, "Blessed is the man that walketh not in the counsel of the ungodly, nor standeth in the way of sinners, nor sitteth in the seat of the scornful" (Ps. 1:1).

There is a process, not progress, in this pattern, for it is a downward movement. When we sit by the enemy's fire, we are in *danger*. If we walk long enough, and stand around for awhile, we will soon look for a comfortable seat. Many an otherwise good person has fallen because he put himself in the wrong place and with the wrong people.

The first time Peter was asked of his association with Jesus, he simply denied it. The second time he was asked, he denied it with an oath. The third time, he denied the association with Jesus with cursing and swearing. First, a simple "no." Then an oath—"I swear on a stack of Bibles." Then the invoking of a curse upon one's self—"I'll be _____ if I know him." It is probable that under the excitement and the pressure of the moment, he relapsed to an earlier habit which had been abandoned through the Savior's teachings. Before he knew it, he had done the very thing he had boasted he would never do. And it happened because he did not understand his tendency to overconfidence, and he picked the wrong companions.

Be careful of the company you keep. Evil companions are more likely to drag you down than you are to lift them up. The person who thinks he can run with the wrong kind of friends and live the right kind of life will come to the same kind of collapse.

As Peter made his third denial, Jesus turned and looked upon him. The memory of Jesus' warning came fresh and

HUMILITY: Overcome by Overconfidence

clear into his mind, and he began to weep bitter tears of remorse. He had discovered the fact that all of us must discover sooner or later; the Master knows us better than we know ourselves.

The Saint Peter Principle is clear: our only hope of spiritual victory in life is that we honestly and humbly acknowledge our own weakness and that we look to Jesus for strength. Our spiritual achievement depends on it.

Notes

1. William Manchester, *American Caesar* (Boston: Little Brown and Company, 1978).
2. Gerald R. Ford, *A Time to Heal* (New York: Harper & Row, 1979), p. 34.
3. Ibid., p. 35.
4. Ibid., p. 35-36.

12
DETERMINATION
Failure Doesn't Have to Be Final

Failure can be a jarring experience. It can rock us on our heels and daze us momentarily. But failure does not have to be final. Defeat does not have to be devastating. Prime Minister Menachem Begin of Israel ran for the office of prime minister nine times before he was elected to the office.

Booth Tarkington wrote short stories for five years before a single story was accepted for publication.

Robert Louis Stevenson's first book was condemned so heartlessly by the critics that Stevenson contemplated suicide.

A reporter called Thomas A. Edison one afternoon when the scientist was attempting to find a substitute for lead in the manufacture of storage batteries. Edison informed the man that he had made one thousand experiments, but none of them had worked. "But aren't you discouraged by all of this waste of effort?" the reporter asked, amazed. "Waste!" exclaimed Mr. Edison. "There is nothing wasted. I have discovered one thousand things that won't work." Eventually, he did find something that would work.

The catalogue of failures by Abraham Lincoln is legendary: failed in business, 1831; defeated for legislature, 1832; failed in business again, 1833; sweetheart died, 1835; suffered nervous breakdown, 1836; defeated for speaker, 1838; defeated for elector, 1840; defeated for Congress, 1848; defeated for Senate, 1855; defeated for vice-president, 1856;

DETERMINATION: Failure Doesn't Have to be Final

defeated for Senate, 1858; elected president of United States, 1860.

Babe Ruth struck out 1,330 times, a record in futility unapproached by any other player in the history of baseball. But that isn't what we remember about Babe Ruth. His 714 home runs obliterated the 1,330 strikeouts.

Cy Young, perhaps the best pitcher of all time, accumulated 511 victories, a mark that never has been threatened. But what is generally forgotten is that Young actually lost almost as many games as he won.

During the French and Indian Wars, at Fort Necessity, a young American officer capitulated to the enemy. But we never think of George Washington as the man who surrendered to the French.

It is true in the spiritual realm as in politics, science, literature, or sports. Failure does not have to be final; defeat does not have to be devastating. If we are ever to attain our highest level in both character and in career, we must remember this.

Jesus taught us this when he told Peter in the upper room, "Satan hath desired to have you, that he may sift you as wheat: but I have prayed for thee, that thy faith fail not; and when thou are converted, strengthen thy brothers" (Luke 22:31-32).

This is a warning to Peter of his approaching denial. Jesus told him that Satan has asked for permission to shake him, and permission had been granted. Then, Jesus assured Peter that he had prayed for him that he would remain faithful. Jesus would not prevent the temptation, but he would pray for Peter not to yield.

However, Jesus knew that Peter would fail. He knew in spite of Peter's protests that "the Rock" would crack under the pressure of temptation. That very night he would deny him three times.

That's when Jesus said this very surprising thing. He said, "When thou art converted, strengthen thy brethren" (Luke 22:31-32). The word *converted* does not refer to Peter's salvation. Jesus was not suggesting that Peter would lose his salvation and then regain it. It means literally "to turn again." During the arrest and trial of Jesus, Peter would turn away from Jesus in fright and denial. In time, he would realize his sin and failure and would weep bitter tears of repentance. Then he would turn back to Jesus to confess his love and devotion and be recommissioned as an apostle. Jesus tells him that when this happens he is to strengthen his brethren.

Jesus knew Peter would yield to the temptations of Satan and would deny him, but he wanted Peter to know that failure did not have to be final. He could come back and be of useful service in the kingdom of God. In fact, as a result of his failure Peter would be better able to help others. He would come back from this experience humbler, wiser, and more understanding. Thus Jesus wanted him to use this experience of failure to help other people.

Jesus didn't have to say that. He could have told Peter, "If you fail me, you are finished. I'll be through with you forever." Or he could have said, "If you fail, you should give up in disgrace and never try again. You should hide in shame and never appear on the pages of history again."

But he didn't. Jesus knew that failure doesn't consist of falling down but in staying down. Defeat does not have to be a disgrace. There is always a second chance, another half to play, and victory can still be snatched from the jaws of defeat. He knew that he could come out of failure better able to help others, and that's what Jesus wanted him to do.

Successful living demands that of us. No one ever achieves his highest potential in life without his share of failures. Unless we learn to capitalize on our failures, we will never become our best selves. What failure did for Peter it can do for you and

DETERMINATION: Failure Doesn't Have to be Final

me. It can teach us some things that we can learn in no other way.

Conquering the King

The first thing failure can teach us is humility. One of Peter's biggest problems was that he trusted too much in his own ability. He suffered from an overdose of overconfidence. He relied on his own strength, and that's why he failed God. This failure punctured his pride. It dented his ego. It made him keenly aware that while his spirit was willing his flesh was weak, and it brought him to his knees in repentance and humility. He realized that he must trust in the Lord rather than in himself.

Pride is the king of all sins. It is the sin that turned the devil into the devil. It is this sin that got Adam and Eve. And it is a constant danger to you and me. Jesus once told a parable about two men who went to the Temple to pray. One was a Pharisee and the other a publican. The Pharisee prayed to himself saying, "God, I thank you that I am not like other men: crooks, dishonest, adulterers. I fast twice a week. I give tithes of everything that I possess. God, I thank you for me" (see Luke 18:10).

The publican stood off in the background and was so ashamed of himself that he would not even lift up his eyes to heaven. In deep distress he prayed "God be merciful to me, a sinner" (Luke 18:13). Then Jesus said that the publican, the man who expressed real humility, was the one who left church justified in God's sight.

He told this parable to teach the proud and arrogant Pharisees the necessity of humility. Luke says that he spoke it unto those who "trusted in themselves that they were righteous, and despised others" (Luke 18:9). That statement indicates that pride always expresses itself in two directions. Vertically, it makes us feel that we do not need God. Horizontally, it makes us look down on other people.

Without humility, we cannot even enter into the kingdom of God. Jesus said, "Blessed are the poor in spirit: for theirs is the kingdom of heaven" (Matt. 5:3). The poor in spirit are opposite to those who are rich in spirit. The word *poor* describes a man who fully realizes his own inadequacy, his worthlessness, his own destitution, and who puts his whole trust in God. It describes a man who realizes that by himself a victorious life is impossible, but with God all things are possible.

Not only is humility essential to salvation, it is also essential to service. One way or the other, we must learn humility if we are to be usable in service. Sometimes in order to teach us humility, God must allow troubles and trials to come into our lives. This was the testimony of the apostle Paul. He often stared death in the face. Concerning these trials he wrote, "We had the sentence of death in ourselves, that we should not trust in ourselves, but in God which raiseth the dead" (2 Cor. 1:9).

On another occasion he told of a nagging ailment that kept him from the pride he might have felt because of a special vision he had from God. We get the idea that humility was not an easy or an automatic virtue for Paul. He saw suffering as keeping him from being proud and making him useful in God's service.

He expressed it this way, "And lest I should be exalted above measure through the abundance of the revelation, there was given me a thorn in the flesh, the messenger of Satan to buffet me, lest I should be exalted above measure" (2 Cor. 12:7). The word *buffet* means to strike with the fist. It is the same word that is used to describe the soldiers as they hit, punched, and jabbed Jesus during the mockery of his trial. The apostle Paul was saying that his infirmities kept him beaten down to his knees in humility and thus kept him useful in God's service.

DETERMINATION: Failure Doesn't Have to be Final

Troubles knock a lot of nonsense out of us. They teach us our own weakness and our need of God. Failure works the same way. We usually learn much more from our defeats than we do from our victories. In victory we tend to celebrate. In our defeats we tend to evaluate. Thus the defeats of life are usually of more value to us than the victories.

Understanding from Ulcers

Not only does failure teach us humility, but it can also teach us sympathy. It can make us more understanding, more accepting, less judgmental, and less condemning of other people. It makes us keenly aware of our own weaknesses and failures and thus more sympathetic toward the weaknesses and failures of other people.

Pride by its very nature is competitive. It not only leads to conceit but to competitiveness. It causes us to look down on others and to criticize them for their faults and failures. It is so easy to develop a critical and caustic attitude toward others until we have had some failures of our own. As someone has said, "In the game of life it is a good idea to have a few early losses, which relieve you of the pressure of trying to maintain an undefeated season." It is only the person who has failed who can understand and accept the failures of others. The Bible teaches us that we ought to have this kind of love and compassion towards others.

Paul spoke of this when he said, "Brethren, if a man be overtaken in a fault, ye which are spiritual, restore such an one in the spirit of meekness; considering thyself, lest thou also be tempted" (Gal. 6:1). When fellow Christians fall into sin we have three options. We can *deplore* them, that is, criticize, condemn, and throw stones at them; *ignore* them, that is, act as though they do not exist; or we can *restore* them, that is, we can put our arms around them and set them on their feet again.

Someone has said that the Christian army is the only army in the world that shoots its own wounded. That's tragically true. But the person who has had the experience of failing himself is far less likely to condemn or to throw stones at others who have failed.

Several years ago I developed an ulcer. That was a shattering blow to my ego. Ulcers are a result of worry and tension, and worry and tension are indications of a lack of faith. I thought I should have more faith than that. I thought I was the kind of person who gave ulcers, not got them! I was so distressed by the blow to my ego that I went into a deep depression. It was as though the light of life had gone out of me. I was in a dark tunnel and could see no light at the end of it.

Prior to that time if you had said to me, "I am depressed," I would likely have said to you, "Just snap out of it." I thought it was that easy. I thought if a person was depressed, all he needed to do was to think happy thoughts, to get involved in good activities, to stop feeling sorry for himself, and his depression would pass. Then I found out from my own experience that it was not that way at all. Out of my own weakness and sin and failure, I learned to be more sympathetic toward other people.

It took me several years before I could muster up enough courage to tell other people about my own depression. When I finally did, I had a steady stream of people coming to me for counseling. They wanted to talk to someone who understood how they felt and who had been where they were. My own failure taught me sympathy. I am much more understanding than I once was.

Failure for me has been a practical working out of the great truth that "all things work together for good to them that love God, . . . who are called according to his purpose" (Rom. 8:28). That verse does not say that God causes everything that happens. He doesn't! Nor does it say that everything that

DETERMINATION: Failure Doesn't Have to be Final

happens is good. It isn't! But it does say that no experience is a total waste when we put it in the hands of God. It says that God can work redemptively even in the failures and frustrations and defeats of life. If we give to him any experience, he is able to bring something good and worthwhile out of it. That's what he did in my case. And he can do that in your life also.

The Greatness of Grace

Not only can failure teach us humility and sympathy, but it can also teach us the greatness of God's grace. It is only the person who has failed and been forgiven, who has stumbled and been picked up, who has been in the mud and then been washed clean, who can understand the depths of God's grace.

I'm sure that Simon Peter always knew of Jesus' love. After all, Jesus expressed confidence in him the very first time they met by telling him he'd become a rock of strength and stability. Later Jesus called him to be one of his twelve apostles. Then for a period of three years he taught him in all kinds of situations.

But he never understood the depths of Christ's love until he denied Jesus. Then he discovered that even though he had denied Christ, still Christ loved him and received him back again as a disciple. That made him aware as nothing else could of God's grace.

One of the most remarkable things about the whole story of Simon's denial and failure is his absolute honesty in the telling of it. If ever there was an incident which one might have expected to be hushed up, this was it. Yet the story is told in all its stark shame in the New Testament.

And the most remarkable part of it is that the story must go back to Peter himself. For no one else was there to have told it. He wanted us to know that his boast had proven vain and that Jesus' prediction had come true. He wanted us to know that the man Jesus called "the Rock" had crumbled under the pressure of temptation. Peter made this incident an essential part of his gospel and did so for the very best reason. Every time he told the story, he could say, "Look at me. Look what I did. And still Jesus forgave me. He forgave me when I failed him in his bitterest hour of need. He took me, Peter, the coward, and used even me. What Jesus did for me, he can surely do for you."

Often it is our failures that give us our testimony. Charles Colson, President Nixon's special counselor and hatchet man, was imprisoned as a result of this Watergate involvement. After his release from prison, he began a prison fellowship to help win convicts to Christ. In a recent letter he said:

> This may sound depressing, but as I look back on the four years I spent in the office next to the president of the United States, I can't remember meeting one person whose life was really affected by the social legislation I worked so hard to bring about. We spent billions to buy results, but it wasn't enough.
>
> Ironically, after the humiliation of the Watergate conviction crumbled my world of influence, I discovered how God can affect thousands of people through the life of one broken person.[1]

Colson discovered the depths of God's grace for himself and for others through his shattered dreams and his crumbled world. It is doubtful if he would ever have discovered it any other way.

Thank God, the story of Simon Peter does not end in failure. After Peter denied Jesus the third time, Jesus turned and looked at him. The look of Jesus was like a dagger piercing Peter's heart, and he went out and wept bitter tears of repentance and remorse. This was the beginning of his recovery and return.

What a contrast between Peter and Judas! Both of them

DETERMINATION: Failure Doesn't Have to be Final

failed Jesus the same night. Judas betrayed Jesus, and Peter denied him. But the end result of these two men was altogether different. One committed suicide; the other wept bitter tears of repentance. One determined his own judgment, and the other accepted the judgment of God. One made failure the end of his life. The other made it the beginning.

Did Jesus not look at Judas, too? I am sure he did when He said to Judas, "Betrayest thou the Son of man with a kiss?" (Luke 22:48). It was the same look and the same love that he gave to Peter. But Judas rejected his love. He was not willing to be helped. Peter responded and repented. How different the outcome!

The crucial question for you and me is, "How will we handle our failures today? Will we handle them as Judas did, or as Peter did?" The only way to handle them is the way Peter did. It is the way of humility and repentance.

Satan sifted Peter to get rid of his faith, but instead he got rid of his self-confidence. If that happens to you, then your failure doesn't have to be final; your defeat doesn't have to be disastrous. You can use your experience to help others. It can give you a testimony. Peter came back from failure to usefulness, and you can too.

Note

1. Charles Colson, *Life Sentence* (Virginia: Chosen Books Publishing Co., Ltd., 1979).

13

REPENTANCE
The Gospel of the Second Chance

On New Year's Day, 1929, Georgia Tech played the University of California in the Rose Bowl. In that game, a man named Roy Riegels recovered a fumble for California, somehow became confused, and started running in the wrong direction. He ran sixty-five yards before one of his own teammates overtook him and tackled him just before he scored for the opposing team. When California attempted to punt, Tech blocked the kick and scored a safety, which was the ultimate margin of victory.

That strange play came in the first half, and everyone who was watching the game was asking the same question, "What will Coach Price do with Roy Riegels in the second half?" The men filed off the field and went into the dressing room to regroup. As usual they sat on the benches and on the floor—all but Riegels. He put a blanket around his shoulder, sat down in a corner with his face in his hands, and wept over his mistake.

As you know, coaches usually have a great deal to say to their team during the halftime. But that day Coach Price was quiet. No doubt, he was trying to decide what to do with Riegels and what to do to turn his team around. Then the timekeeper came in and announced that there were three minutes before playing time. Coach Price looked at his team and said simply, "Men, the same team that played the first half will start the second half."

The players got up and started out—all but Riegels. He did

REPENTANCE: The Gospel of the Second Chance   133

not budge. The coach looked back and called to him again; still he did not move. Then Coach Price went over where Riegels sat and said, "Roy, didn't you hear me? The same team that played the first half will start the second."

Then Roy Riegels looked up, his cheeks wet with a strong man's tears, and said, "Coach, I can't do it to save my life. I've ruined you. I've ruined the University of California. I've ruined myself. I couldn't face that crowd in the stadium to save my life." Then Coach Price reached out and put his hand on Riegels' shoulder and said to him; "Roy, get up and go back; the game is only half over."

Roy Riegels did go back on to the field, and those who watched the game that day will tell you that they have never seen a man play football like he did that second half.

There are times when all of us, like Roy Riegels, get mixed up, confused, and run in the wrong direction. There are times when we fail our friends, ourselves, and even our Lord. When we do, we might expect the Lord to leave us in the locker room of self-pity or to place us on the bench of inactivity. But instead he comes to us to say, "Get up and go on back on to the playing field; the game is only half over. You still have a chance to snatch victory from the jaws of defeat." At the moment of our greatest defeat, we discover that the gospel is good news for failures. It is the gospel of the second chance.

If we are ever to achieve our highest potential in both character and career, we must learn this. We have to get up from failure and self-pity and get back into fellowship and service. The grace of God makes this possible.

There is a flesh and blood demonstration of this in the life of Simon Peter. Despite his miserable performance during the trial and crucifixion of Jesus, he was not only forgiven but reinstated to service. We sometimes make the distinction that a glaring failure may permanently disqualify a person from further service even though his sin may be forgiven by God.

Jesus, however, did not accept this. He was willing to reinstate Peter to his apostleship and to entrust him with a ministry to other people.

Following his denial of Jesus, Peter was completely devastated emotionally and spiritually. He went out and wept bitter tears of regret. Then there followed the crucifixion and three days of darkness and despair before Jesus was resurrected from the grave. What glorious good news the resurrection was to the disciples! In the days that followed, Jesus showed himself many times to them. They knew he was alive. No one could doubt that, but they did not understand the full meaning of it yet. During the next forty days, there occurred the matchless wonder of his appearing and disappearing. They never knew when they might see him next. He came and went without announcement or explanation. This left the disciples with an uncertain and perplexed feeling. They were restless, disturbed. Nothing seemed settled.

Then it was that Simon, the man of action, said in effect, "I cannot bear this; I must do something. I am going fishing" (see John 21:3). The others joined him and said, "We are coming, too."

So the disciples went back to the Sea of Galilee to fish. They toiled all night long and caught nothing. Towards the dawn, they headed to the shore. As they neared it, Peter saw a figure silhouetted against the eastern sky. He immediately recognized it as Jesus. Without waiting for the boat to dock, he plunged into the water, and swam ashore. There he found Jesus cooking breakfast for the disciples over an open fire. When the others arrived, they ate in restrained silence. And no one was quieter than Peter. The memory of his cursing and denial was still fresh in his mind, so what could he say in the presence of these other men?

It was a merciful relief when Jesus invited Peter to walk with him. As they walked along the Sea of Galilee, Jesus asked,

REPENTANCE: The Gospel of the Second Chance 135

"Simon, son of Jonas, lovest thou me more than these?" Peter answered, "Yes, Lord, I love you." Jesus then said to him, "Feed my lambs." Then Jesus asked him the same question the second time. Again Peter affirmed his love for Jesus. And again Jesus commissioned him to feed his sheep.

The third time Jesus asked him the same question. It grieved Peter in his heart that Jesus should ask him this same question three times. However, he responded by saying, "Lord, thou knowest all things; thou knowest that I love thee." And again Jesus said, "Feed my sheep" (John 21:15-17).

At this point, Jesus recalls Peter to his apostleship by saying, "Follow me." Those are the same words that he had spoken to him three years earlier when he had found him washing his nets by the Sea of Galilee (Matt. 4:19).

With this experience, Peter was back in complete fellowship and service once again. He had made the full circle in his life. He was back where he had started, but he was back a stronger, a wiser, and a more mature man. This kind of recovery is possible for every person who has failed God, others, and even himself. The experience of Peter teaches us the essential steps on the road which we must all travel from time to time—the road back to fellowship and usefulness.

These three steps back to Christ are confession, contrition, and commitment.

The Step of Confession

The road back to usefulness for Peter started with confession—the confession of love. As he and Jesus talked, Jesus did not chide him, reprove him, or condemn him. He rather probed his heart to discover the depth of his love. Jesus seems to be far more interested in his confession of love and devotion than he is in his confession of sin.

The reason for this is simple. Sin is not just breaking the

commandments of God. It is breaking the heart of God. Sin, by its very nature, is not only against law but also against love. If there is to be a recovery in the fullest sense of the word, there must be more than an acknowledgment of sin. There must also be an acknowledgment of love and devotion.

And it cannot be merely a casual love. It has to be a superior love. Jesus' first question reveals this. He said, "Simon, son of Jonas, lovest thou me more than these?" (John 21:15). That phrase "more than these" is an interesting one. It has been the subject of a great deal of speculation and debate ever since it was written.

What did Jesus mean by these words?

Some have suggested that they have reference to the fishing paraphernalia that was nearby. They believed that Jesus was saying, "Simon, do you love me more than you love these boats and these nets?" Peter had been a fisherman by trade before Jesus had called him to be an apostle. The boats and nets represented his old way of life. They represented his former occupation, and they represented his principle form of recreation. It may be that Jesus was saying, "Do you love me more than you love your old way of life? Do you love me more than you love your profession? Do you love me more than you love your favorite recreation?"

Others have suggested that the phrase "more than these" has reference to the other disciples. They suggest that Jesus was saying, "Simon, do you love me more than you love these other men?" His brother Andrew was in that group. James and John, his old fishing partners, were also a part of it. And the rest of the men had been his closest companions during the past three years. They had been through the kinds of experiences that weld men into a brotherhood. Perhaps Jesus was saying, "Simon, do you love me more than you love your brother? Do you love me more than you love your business associates? Do you love me more than you love your dearest friends?"

REPENTANCE: The Gospel of the Second Chance

Others have suggested that by the phrase "more than these" Jesus was saying, "Simon, do you love me more than these other men love me?" There was a time when Peter had boasted of that. In the upper room after Jesus had announced that "all ye shall be offended because of me" (Matt. 26:31), Peter, in his impulsiveness, had blurted out, "Lord, it won't be me. These other men may forsake you, but I will be true to you even unto death" (see Matt. 26:33). It was then that Jesus had told Peter that he would deny him three times that very night.

The prophecy of Jesus had come true, and Peter had failed the Lord miserably. Jesus may very well be saying here, "Peter, you once boasted that your loyalty was greater than that of these other men. Now I ask you again, 'Do you love me more than these other men love me?' "

We can never be completely sure what Jesus meant by the phrase "more than these." However, we can be sure of one thing. Whatever he had reference to, Jesus was saying, "I want you to love me more than anyone or anything else." That's the kind of love he wants. That's the kind of confession he demands from us.

The road to recovery is never easy or automatic. It demands a superior love and loyalty to Jesus Christ, or there can be no return.

The Step of Contrition

While a love for Christ is essential, it is not sufficient. There must also be a deep contrition over sin. David learned this out of his bitter experience of sin and repentance. He wrote out of his recovery experience, "For thou desirest not sacrifice; else would I give it: thou delightest not in burnt offering. The sacrifices of God are a broken spirit: a broken and a contrite heart, O God, thou wilt not despise" (Ps. 51:16-17).

The road back to fellowship and service is always drenched

with tears. The grief of Peter was both immediate and continual. Peter had no sooner denied Jesus than the rooster crowed, and he remembered Jesus' warning. That was enough to break his heart. He went out and wept bitterly.

Tradition tells us that Peter never again heard a rooster crow without having tears come to his eyes. When he met Jesus again, he was still grieving over his sin in this experience. The Bible says, "Peter was grieved because he said unto him the third time, Lovest thou me?" (John 21:17).

Why was Peter grieved? The threefold question was a reminder of his threefold denial. Grief is often the price we pay for the haunting memory of failure. But there is a second reason for his grief that is not readily apparent in the English translations of the experience. The full force of this conversation is felt only in the Greek language. There are two different words for love used in this passage. One is a strong word that describes the highest kind of spiritual devotion (*agapao*). The second is a weaker form of love that indicates a warm affection (*phileo*). The first two times Jesus asks Peter if he loves him, he uses the stronger of these two words. But, in his reply, Peter is afraid to use that strong word. His failure at the trial of Jesus had taken away his egotism and his sense of self-sufficiency. So he responds with the weaker word for love. It is a response that shows his new spirit of humility.

So, the third time, Jesus questions Peter about his love he uses that same weaker word. It is as if Jesus is saying, "Well, by your own definition, do you even like me?" That is what grieved Peter. He realizes how far he has fallen, and he is deeply disappointed not only in his sin but in himself.

There can be no spiritual recovery without a sense of sorrow over sin. Someone once asked Lincoln how he felt after losing an election. He said, "I felt like the little boy who stubbed his toe. I was too old to cry, and it hurt too much to laugh." We are never too old to cry. And when we stub our toe spiritually,

REPENTANCE: The Gospel of the Second Chance

we need to confess not only our love for Jesus but also our grief over sin.

The Step of Commitment

It is at this point that Jesus said to Peter, "Follow me." He is calling for a new commitment in service and in obedience. It is essentially the same call that Jesus had issued to him three years earlier by the Sea of Galilee.

Love and guilt are both compelling forces. Many a stained-glass window has been put in a church as a result of guilt over sin. But love has also sparked many a noble deed. Jesus is appealing to this higher and nobler motive when he calls on Peter to follow him again.

The acceptance of this call would prove costly. Jesus here, as always, spells out the potential danger. No one could ever accuse Jesus of calling men under false pretenses. He reminds Peter that in his younger years he was free and self-willed. But in the days ahead he would stretch forth his hands [on the cross] and another would gird [fasten] him, and would carry him where he didn't want to go [to the place of execution] (see John 21:18).

This is suitable language for crucifixion. He is telling Peter of his future martyrdom if he accepts the call to discipleship.

As Jesus and Peter are walking, Peter turns to see John following close behind. He then says to Jesus, "You have just spoken to me about my death. Now, what about John? What's going to happen to him?" Jesus replied sharply, "If I will that John remains alive until I come again, what is that to you? I want you to follow me."

Jesus is saying, in effect, "Peter, regardless of your past failures, regardless of the sacrifices you may have to make, and regardless of what other people may do, I am calling you to follow me." It is only as he is willing to make this kind of total commitment that he can come back into fellowship and service with the Master.

Following Jesus can be a costly experience. The Book of Acts described those earlier missionaries Paul and Silas as men who "hazarded their lives for the name of our Lord Jesus Christ" (Acts 15:26). The word *hazarded* is a gambling term. It means "to risk, to wager, to lay something on the line." Those early followers of Christ laid their lives on the line for him and the gospel. Unless we are willing to do the same, we will never realize our full potential in either character or in career. Some unknown poet has said:

> I wish there was some wonderful place
>   Called the land of Beginning Again
> Where all our mistakes, and all our heartaches
>   And all of our selfish griefs
> Could be cast like a shabby old coat at the door
>   And never put on again.

There is such a place. It is at the foot of the cross of Christ. To get there requires that you come to Christ in confession, contrition, and recommitment, but it is worth the price. Peter began again and so can you. You can get up from your past failures and go on to become all God wants you to be. This is a part of the Saint Peter Principle. This is the gospel of the second chance.

14
POWER
A Rock-Man At Last

A group of college students were sitting in the lounge of their student center on a state campus. Somehow the conversation turned toward the future and what they hoped to be several years from then. One mentioned that she hoped to be a teacher. Another remarked he wanted to be an accountant. Another said he wanted to be an architect. Several were undecided. One young lady seemed to be deep in thought. When at last she was asked what she hoped to be one day, she startled everyone by replying, "I hope to be a saint."

This is God's goal for every one of us. He wants us to become Christlike in our character and servants in our careers. It is his desire that every one of us achieve our highest potential in all that we are and in all that we do. He wants to mold us into what we are capable of being and develop us into what we are capable of doing. The life of Peter the apostle is a good illustration of this.

The Gospels are full of the acts of Peter. After the Lord's himself, Peter's name is mentioned more often than any other. Repeatedly in them we find Jesus teaching, training, correcting, and forgiving Peter as he leads him on toward reaching his full possibilities. However, the Gospels end with Simon far from what he ought to be. In fact, they end with Peter as a dismal failure. Having boasted of his loyalty to Jesus, he then sinks to his lowest depths of failure by completely denying that he even knew the Lord.

Only John records the fact that following this disgraceful denial, Jesus reinstates Peter to his apostleship and recommissions him to his original task. If all we had of the life of Peter were contained in the Gospels, we would be forced to question the judgment of Jesus. We would have to say, "Lord, you goofed on this one." For Peter was nowhere near the rock in character nor a witness in career that Jesus had said he would become.

The Rock Solidified

However, if you read on in the Book of Acts, you discover that Peter becomes a changed man. The prediction and promise of Jesus comes true. After Jesus' ascension, at which he "sent out" his apostles into the world, Peter at once assumed the leadership of the apostles. He suggested the choice of a replacement for Judas. He spoke for the apostles on the day of Pentecost and courageously declared that the Jesus whom the people had crucified was both Lord and Savior. The result was that three thousand people were converted to faith in Christ. He was the first of the apostles to perform a miracle in the name of Jesus. He healed the crippled man at the Beautiful Gate of the Temple. He conducted the defense of John and himself before the Sanhedrin. He boldly accused the very same men who had Jesus crucified of being guilty of the crime of the ages, and he told them that unless they repented and turned in faith to Christ there was no hope for them.

When Ananias and Sapphira lied about their giving, Peter pronounced the condemnation of God upon them. He was soon renowned for his miracles done in the name of Jesus. When the great revival broke out in Samaria, he and John were sent as representatives of the apostles to see if it was the authentic work of God. And through the laying on of their hands, the Holy Spirit came to the baptized believers they found there.

POWER: A Rock-Man at Last

It was Peter who healed Aeneas, the paralytic, at Lydda, and who raised to life Dorcas, the woman of Joppa renowned for her good works. While in Joppa (now Jaffa), Peter received a vision convincing him that "God is no respecter of persons, but that in every nation those who fear him and do what is right are acceptable to him" (see Acts 10:34-35). He then went to the home of Cornelius, a Roman centurion, and preached the gospel to him and his household, and they were all converted to Christ and then baptized. Later at the great council of Jerusalem, he defended the inclusion of uncircumcised Gentiles in the Christian movement. When Herod declared war on the church, Peter was arrested and thrown in jail. After he was miraculously released from jail by an angel, he then disappeared from the narrative in the Book of Acts.

Peter is so prominent in the early chapters of the Book of Acts that someone has suggested that Acts 1-12 ought to be named "The Acts of Simon Peter." In these pages we see him as solid and steadfast. He is a rock of commitment, conviction, consistence, and courage. And he is witnessing for Christ everywhere. When he preaches, thousands are saved. He does all of this in the face of the greatest of obstacles. Repeatedly he is arrested and interrograted, threatened, beaten, and imprisoned. At least three times in the first twelve chapters in the Book of Acts, Peter is arrested and imprisoned for preaching the gospel of Jesus Christ.

Not once does he play the coward; not once does he run; not once does he deny Jesus. But he boldly declares that Jesus Christ is Lord. When he is commanded to stop preaching in the name of Jesus he said, "We cannot help but preach the things we have seen and heard . . . we must obey God rather than men."

Peter, the lambhearted, has become Peter, the lionhearted. He is a man of bold conviction who cannot be shaken from what he believes. There are not many people like that.

One day a senator, dealing with a hot issue, came to see

Franklin Delano Roosevelt. The Senator expressed his views to the president with great enthusiasm. When he finished, the president said, "That's right, absolutely right, you're 100 percent right." And the man thanked him and left. In just a matter of a few moments, another senator came in and was just as strong and as enthusiastic with the opposite point of view. The president listened to him patiently and kindly, and when he had finished he said, "Senator, that's right, absolutely right, you're 100 percent right." The Senator thanked him and left.

Then Eleanor came in and said, "Why, Franklin, do you realize what you have done? One of those men came in and said one thing, and the other one said exactly the opposite, and you told them both that they were right, absolutely right, 100 percent right. And, Franklin, you know that that was a lie." And he said, "Eleanor, that's right, absolutely right, you are 100 percent right." Well, that's the way many of us deal with problems.

Recently a man created a new and useful word, *catmatic*. It is the opposite of dogmatic. A catmatic person is one who "pussyfoots" around. No one could ever accuse Peter of pussyfooting around. Now with great boldness and conviction, he declared what he believed to be true.

And he sealed his conviction with his life. By the year AD 64, Nero had begun the persecution of Christians throughout the Empire. In that year, he burned the city of Rome so that he could rebuild it as a monument to himself. The Roman historian Tacitus states that everyone in Rome believed the great fire had been set on the orders of the emperor. He continues,

> Nero set up as the culprits and punished with the utmost refinement of cruelty a class hated for their admonitions, who were commonly called Christians . . . besides being put to death, they were made to serve as objects of amusements; they were clad in the hides of beasts and

POWER: A Rock-Man at Last

torn to death by dogs; others were crucified; others set on fire to serve to illumine the night when daylight failed.

These were times when it could hurt to be a Christian. And Peter was to find this out from experience. For tradition has preserved in the noncanonical *Acts of Peter*, chapter 35, (written 150 years after his death) that in the full knowledge of his danger Peter journeyed to Rome to hearten the endangered Christian community. As the number of deaths increased, those who remained implored Peter to escape so that his leadership might be spared for other churches who needed him. Under the pressure he agreed and fled down the Appian Way. But he was abruptly halted by a vision of Jesus walking toward the Eternal City.

Peter asked, "Where are you going, Lord?"

Jesus answered, "To Rome, to be crucified there."

Remembering poignantly, as though it were but the day before, how he had once denied and deserted Jesus in his extremity, Peter turned about and went back to share the lot of his fellow-Christians.

Finally, he was apprehended and condemned to death by crucifixion. Feeling himself unworthy to die as the Lord had died, he asked if he could be crucified upside down. Thus he died a martyr's death for the cause of Christ. He was willing to seal with his blood that which he had proclaimed with his lips.

What a change had taken place in this man! The man who had once tried to divert Jesus from the cross was now proclaiming that the cross was the only way of redemption. The man who in anger had cut off the ear of a soldier who had come to arrest Jesus was now proclaiming that forgiveness and salvation were available to the very people who had crucified the Lord. The man who had cowardly run to hide in the night and denied his Lord was now risking life and limb to spread the gospel everywhere.

Peter had become the man Christ had predicted he would become. The sand had solidified. He was now a rock of commitment, conviction, consistency, and courage. He had achieved his highest potential in both character and in career. The Saint Peter Principle had worked.

What Made the Difference?

How are we to account for this change in the life of Peter? Of course, the three years that he had companied with Jesus did something to him and in him. But it had not brought about the change that Jesus had predicted. Although Peter had walked by the side of Christ for three years, and he had even made the great confession, he would not at the trial admit he knew Christ. So what brought about the change? It was not just walking with Jesus, nor witnessing the crucifixion, nor viewing the empty tomb.

In those three years with Jesus the fuel had been laid on the fire, but it was not yet lit. The seed had been sown, but it had not yet germinated. All the possibilities of change in Peter had been created, but the change had not yet happened.

What did change him? The New Testament gives the answer when it says, "And they were all filled with the Holy Ghost" (Acts 2:4). It was not until Pentecost that he was changed. It was not until the Spirit had come upon him in power that his cowardice was changed to courage; his unbelief became a flaming faith and conviction that nothing on earth could shake; jealousy was swallowed up in brotherly love; self-interest was killed and became a ministry to others; fear was vanished, and he was afraid of no man . . . no threat . . . no danger.

The only resource of the Christian life is Jesus Christ. We must remember this lest we think we can change ourselves. There is always the danger that we will think that by grim determination and firm resolutions we can change ourselves into what we ought to be, that we can achieve our highest potential by self-effort. But we do not try long until we realize that what we need is not a boost from beneath. We need a birth from above. We need not what we can do, but what God can do.

Our only hope for change is in God's power. We are oftentimes like the young woodpecker who flew out to his first tree. He picked the tallest, straightest pine he could find in the forest and started pecking away. Just as he started pecking away, lightning struck and split the tree right straight down the middle. The shock dazed him, and he flew off with his wings wobbling and his tail feathers smoking saying, "Wow, I didn't know I had it in me."

We don't have the ability in us to change on our own. The power is in the Lord Jesus and in him alone. He is the only one who can make a real difference in our life.

The Source of Our Hope

Therein lies our hope. We have not seen Jesus as Peter did. We have never heard the sound of his voice, we have never seen the sunlight dance on his hair, and we have never traced his footprints in the sands of Galilee as Peter did. But we have the same opportunity to be changed because the same Holy Spirit is available to us today. He has sent his Spirit into the world to lead us in all truth, to convict us of sin, and to be our helper and our guide. Through the indwelling Holy Spirit we are able to achieve our highest potential.

The book *American Caesar* tells of General Douglas MacArthur's liberation of the Philippines in the concluding months of World War II. In 1961 he made a farewell trip to the Philippines to celebrate the fifteenth anniversary of its independence.

He was moved to tears when he discovered that the government had kept a postwar vow that the name of Douglas MacArthur would never be permitted to die among the soldiers of the Republic of the Philippines. It was heard every day when a roll was called, and a sergeant always responded: "Present in spirit."

As a result of the crucifixion, resurrection, ascension, and coming of the Holy Spirit, now every Christian can know that Christ is "present in Spirit" in him. With Jesus Christ in us there is the possibility of achieving our greatest effectiveness in life. Christ in us is our hope of glory.

Those of us who follow Christ never tire of looking at portraits of Peter because he is so thoroughly human. He reminds us so much of ourselves.

Peter is a good lesson to all of us on how human frailty though weak can become strong, and the fearful can be made bold. There is both encouragement and hope in his life. We keep remembering that, if this unstable and undependable man could be changed into a person with a rocklike character and if he could be changed from an obscure fisherman into a worldwide witness for Christ, it can happen to us also. This is the crux of the Saint Peter Principle.

The world has yet to see what God can do with a life completely yielded to him. Why don't you become that person? The secret of transformation is the mighty Spirit who at Pentecost became the believer's reservoir of unfailing power, courage, and wisdom. Yield yourself fully and completely to him today, and the Lord through his indwelling spirit will bring you to your highest potential in both your character and your career.

15
ENDURANCE
The Peter Principle and Saint Peter

One of the ironies of history is that men have applied the Peter Principle to Saint Peter. The Peter Principle is that in a hierarchy people tend to be promoted to a level beyond their competency. Through the years the religious hierarchy has elevated Peter to the office of Pope. The Pope, as you know, is said to be infallible when speaking of matters of faith and ethics. Peter could never be that. Infallibility was clearly beyond his point of competency. Until the end of his life, he was always failing, always stumbling, always sinning. He was anything but infallible. In fact at the last glimpse we have of Peter in Scripture, he is playing the hypocrite. Paul tells us about this in Galatians 2:11-16.

Peter had come to the city of Antioch which by this time had become the center of the Christian movement. The Christian community there had become the base of world mission. It was natural then that Peter, the most influential leader of the church at that time, would go there to visit.

The church at Antioch was made up of both Jewish and Gentile believers. As a part of their community life, the Christians regularly met in homes to share a common meal together. This common meal was called the love feast or the *agape* meal. And it was usually concluded by the observance of the Lord's Supper. Naturally, Peter, when he went to Antioch, participated in these common meals and times of Christian fellowship.

There was a time when such fellowship would have been out of the question, for there had long existed a deep cleavage between the Jews and Gentiles. They had no dealings with one another. In fact, the Jews believed that if they ate with a Gentile they would defile themselves. It simply was not done.

However, through a series of events, God made it clear to Peter and the other Christians that this prejudice and these man-made distinctions had been abolished through the cross of Christ. The Lord led Peter to the home of Cornelius, a Roman soldier who was wanting to know God. As Peter preached the gospel to all those present, the Holy Spirit came on them, and they were every one saved. There could be no doubt about that. These Gentiles had been genuinely converted by faith in Christ alone. When many of the Jewish brethren heard of this, they "glorified God" (Acts 11:18) and acknowledged that he had granted repentance and eternal life to the Gentiles also.

The Cornelius incident opened the door to a worldwide missionary effort to the Gentiles. So Paul and Barnabas went into the Gentile world with full force. God crowned their efforts with great success, and thousands of Gentiles turned to God through faith in Jesus Christ. However, there was still a group of legalistic Jews who held on to their ancient taboos. They were not sure that Gentiles could be saved at all. But if they could be, they would surely have to be circumcised first. They believed that Judaism was the door to Christianity.

As a result of their efforts, great controversy continued to whirl around this issue. So a council was convened in Jerusalem with all of the apostles and elders present to settle the issue once and for all. The end result was that after prayer and testimonies they affirmed again the fact that salvation was offered to all men on the same basis—by faith in Christ alone. The distinctions between Jews and Gentiles had all been abol-

ENDURANCE: The Peter Principle and Saint Peter 151

ished in Christ. God was no respecter of persons, and neither should his people be.

So it was with this new sense of liberty that Peter went to Antioch and freely ate with both Jews and Gentiles in these fellowship meals. However, some of the legalistic Jews still refused to surrender their old prejudices. In time, some of them came from Jerusalem to Antioch and were highly critical of Peter's association with Gentiles. When Peter learned of their criticism, he stopped associating with the Gentile converts. Bit by bit he withdrew himself from fellowship with them. Another person of less renown might have done what Peter did and hardly been noticed. But not Peter. He was conspicuous by his absence. And everyone knew why he was no longer attending their meetings.

What made matters worse was that Peter's actions had a far-reaching effect. Other Jewish Christians followed his example, and they quit participating in the fellowship meals also. In fact, even Barnabas was influenced by Peter's actions, and he, too, quit attending them. This was a real shock to the apostle Paul. After all, it had been Barnabas who had first introduced him to the Jewish Christians in Jerusalem. It had been Barnabas who had sought him out and invited him to join in the great missionary effort in Antioch. It had been Barnabas who had been his strong companion of the first missionary journey. It had been Barnabas who had supported him in his stand at the Jerusalem conference. Now Barnabas, one of the most respected leaders in the Christian community, was following Peter's example and was separating himself from fellowship with the Gentile believers.

This was potentially an explosive situation. You can easily see how the Christian church could be split asunder by it. The apostle Paul could not allow this to go on unchecked. So, he tells us in Galatians 2:11-16 that when this happened he withstood Peter to his face. He publicly called him on the carpet and described his activities as hypocritical. Twice in this passage of Scripture Paul uses the verb *dissemble*, or *dissimulation*, to describe Peter's actions. The verb literally means "to play act." It means to be a hypocrite. It means to conceal one's real character and feeling so as to appear to be something different.

That's what Peter was doing. He was pretending that his actions stemmed from loyalty to Moses' law. But he knew better. They really stemmed from his fear of the criticism of these legalistic Jews. Peter knew what was right, but he was afraid that he would lose the goodwill of these radical Jews. So under false pretense he reversed his previous practices and dropped out of the Christian meetings.

He took his eyes off the Lord momentarily and put them on men. When he did, the old cowardly fear that had caused him to deny the Lord at Jesus' trial returned. The old tendency to vacillate and compromise came to the surface again, and Peter played the hypocrite.

Can you believe that? Peter, the rock; Peter, the pillar of the church; Peter, the leader of the apostles, is now playing the hypocrite. After three years of walking and talking with Jesus, after being a part of some of the most miraculous experiences of history, the rock has cracked, and he is playing the hypocrite. It is hard to believe! From this experience, there are some important truths for you and me today.

Christians Aren't Perfect

The first thing Peter's hypocrisy teaches us is that Christians aren't perfect; they are just forgiven. If anything ought to make this clear to us it is this experience. Peter, the undisputed leader of the New Testament church; Peter, who preached at Pentecost and saw three thousand people saved;

ENDURANCE: The Peter Principle and Saint Peter

Peter, who preached again and saw five thousand accept the Lord; Peter, who had had miraculous experience after miraculous experience, was now playing the hypocrite. He had succumbed to the pressure of the unbelieving Jews, and he was living contrary to his convictions.

The truth is that the best of men sometimes do the worst of things. None of us are ever beyond the reach of peer pressure. None of us are ever so strong, so mature, so experienced in our Christian faith that we cannot play the hypocrite.

Peter's hypocrisy also shows us just how human these early Christians were. We are prone to suppose that they were well nigh perfect. But they weren't! And neither will we ever be. Aleksandr Solzhenitsyn, in *The Gulag Archipelago,* wrote,

> If only there were evil people somewhere insidiously committing evil deeds, and it were necessary only to separate them from the rest of us and destroy them. But the line dividing good and evil cuts through the heart of every human being. And who is willing to destroy a piece of his own heart?[1]

The fact is that there is no such thing as some people who are good and others who are bad. All people are mixtures. The potential for evil lies in the hearts of all of us. And we never get to the point where we are beyond the reach of sin.

It's important that we remember the fact that Christians aren't perfect, only forgiven. If we don't, we will misunderstand what the church is supposed to be. The church is not a place for good people to go. It is a place for sinners. As the hospital is for the sick, so the church is for the sinful. We should be under no illusions about what we are. We do not attend church because we are perfect; we attend church because we are imperfect. We are forgiven sinners seeking to become all that God wants us to be.

The church is like a family. Families are often made up of

people at various levels of maturity. In a family, there are apt to be little children and teenagers as well as adults. No reasonable person expects all of these people to act alike. Some of them are much more mature than others. And we realize that it is a part of the function of a family to help children and young people grow to full maturity.

The church is the same way. There are some people in it who are in their spiritual infancy. There are others who are spiritual adolescents. And there are others who are well on their way to spiritual maturity. But none of them are perfect. It is only as we understand that Christians are people who have been forgiven of their sins and are in the process of growing to be like Jesus Christ that we can understand and appreciate the church more.

We need to understand this not only in order to accept one another but also in order to accept ourselves. It is so easy to become disappointed and discouraged with yourself in the process of Christian living. You may start out to follow Jesus Christ with the highest resolve only to fall to the lowest depths of discouragement. You may even think, "I guess I'm not a Christian at all" or "Surely God can't use a failure like me." But don't despair. Don't give up. Christians aren't perfect; they are just forgiven.

Sin Is Not to Be Condoned

The second truth in Peter's experience with hypocrisy is that sin is not to be condoned even in the life of a great man. Wrong is wrong, no matter who does it. A famous name does not justify an infamous act.

When Peter, the pillar of the church, played the hypocrite, it was wrong, and someone needed to tell him so. It must have been very difficult for the apostle Paul to withstand this prominent leader to his face, but it had to be done. Peter was in

ENDURANCE: The Peter Principle and Saint Peter

error, and he was leading other people into error also. He could not be allowed to go on in it.

No man is above sin, and no man is above being rebuked for his sin.

Well, I'm telling you, you're no different from anybody else. The Bible declares, "There is no difference: For all have sinned, and come short of the glory of God" (Rom. 3:22-23). Again it says, "There is not a just man upon the earth, that doeth good, and sinneth not" (Eccl. 7:20). In regards to sin we are all alike. Men may differ as to the degree of their sin, but they do not differ in the fact of sin.

Sin in your life or in mine is not to be coddled. It is not to be overlooked. It is never to be condoned.

Falling into Grace

What happens when Christians sin? Do they lose their salvation? Peter's experience with hypocrisy shows us that when Christians sin, they don't fall from grace; they fall into grace. When we see Peter playing the hypocrite after all of his marvelous experiences, we are prompted to ask the Lord, "How long are you going to put up with such inconsistency? When are you going to wash your hands of this man? He seems to be such a hopeless case."

We may even think that Peter had fallen from grace. But the truth of the matter is that when Peter did wrong, the Lord didn't disown him. He did not fall from grace. He fell into grace. For God sent the apostle Paul to reprove him and correct him. He was wrong, and he knew it. His own actions indicted him. We can almost see Peter with his head bowed and his face red admitting that Paul is right, and that he is wrong. And with that humble admission, he becomes a better and more useful servant of Jesus Christ.

Even though Peter sinned against God and played the

hypocrite, he still came back to be blessed and to be a blessing. It was after this failure that he dictated his memoirs to Mark. These notes became the basis for the Gospel of Mark, the first written account of the life of Jesus that the world was to have. And still later he wrote the Epistles of 1 Peter and 2 Peter, two of the greatest books ever written. No, Peter didn't fall from grace when he sinned; he fell *into* grace.

This great truth is not to encourage us to sin. It is to encourage us to remain teachable in spite of our sin. Here's Peter, the pillar of the church, struggling to live right till the end of his life. In this last glimpse we have of him in Scripture, he is still struggling, still growing, still failing, still becoming. It will be the same with us. The road to spiritual achievement is always under construction. We never have it made. We are always striving, never completely arriving at maturity. So don't get discouraged. Don't give up. If God stayed with Peter, he'll stay with you also.

The Saint Peter Principle never suggests that Christians will become perfect and eventually rise above the temptations and trials of life. If says rather that through commitment to Christ we can attain our highest potential in both character and career. We can become all that we have it in us to be. We can reach our greatest effectiveness in God's service.

If that is your desire, they why don't you apply the Saint Peter Principle to your own life? Commit your life to Jesus as Lord and Savior and begin to follow him in faith and obedience. If you will, it will be for you, as it was for Peter, the beginning of achieving your highest spiritual potential.

Note

1. Aleksandr Solzhenitsyn, *The Gulag Archipelago, 1918-1956* (New York: Harper & Row, 1975).